Delphiniums

David and Shirley Bassett

Delphiniums

Timber Press

Photographs © David and Shirley Bassett 2006

ISBN 978-0-88192-800-6

Reproduction by Anorax Imaging Ltd, Leeds, UK
Printed and bound by WKT Co Ltd, China

Published in North America in 2007
by Timber Press, Inc.
The Haseltine Building
133 SW Second Avenue, Suite 450
Portland, Oregon 97204-3527, USA
www.timberpress.com

A catalog record for this title is available from the Library of Congress

Contents

Part 1: KNOWING DELPHINIUMS

1. Introducing Delphiniums

Delphiniums probably first became of interest to humans not for their flowers, but when it was appreciated that potions prepared from the plant could be used to treat aches and pains and to control parasites, such as lice, that made life a misery. The advantages of having the plant material nearby perhaps then led to delphiniums being cultivated around the places where people lived. At a later stage it was appreciated that the flowers are beautiful, and the process began of selecting plants with the most attractive blooms for further cultivation. The familiar delphiniums in gardens today result from hundreds of years of this cultivation process, during which Europeans discovered wild delphiniums in faraway places and used them for plant development by combining them with familiar varieties. Given this intensive mixing of genes, it is hardly surprising that it is now difficult to trace the ancestry of modern delphiniums in terms of the different wild species that have been involved.

What is a Delphinium?

Before going further, we should consider what features of plants belonging to the genus *Delphinium* distinguish them from other plants. We note first that delphiniums – along with some fifty other genera – belong to the family Ranunculaceae and thus have some affinity to other familiar garden flowers such as anemones, aconitums, aquilegias, clematis, hellebores and buttercups. The number and form of the various components of the flower are crucial in differentiating delphiniums from these plants, and in this the characteristic spur on the back of the flower is of major significance. This spur gives flower buds the dolphin-like shape that led to the plants being called 'delphiniums' (from the Greek *delphis*, meaning dolphin) and is also

celebrated in their other common name, larkspur (mirrored literally in the French name, *pied d'alouette*, while the German *Rittersporne* means 'knight's spur').

Flower Structure

A point that easily causes confusion in relation to the components of a delphinium flower is that almost everyone in conversation calls the large colourful bracts 'petals', just as one does for a rose. This is not technically correct because when the delphinium flower bud opens, the leaf scales (sepals) that enclose the flower do not fold back and wither away, as those of a rose bud do. Instead, they expand into the showiest components of the flower, with the much smaller petals forming the central eye. This easily goes unnoticed when looking at the flowers of cultivated delphiniums, which have been bred to emphasize the sepals. However, in some wild delphiniums, such as *D. decorum*, green spots on the outside of the opening flower make it obvious that the bracts are not the true petals, which can, rather, be seen inside above the stamens (see **Figure 1.1**). A prominent green patch or lump

RIGHT: **Figure 1.1.** An opening bud of *D. decorum* clearly shows that the purple bracts, with green patches on the outside, are sepals, not petals.

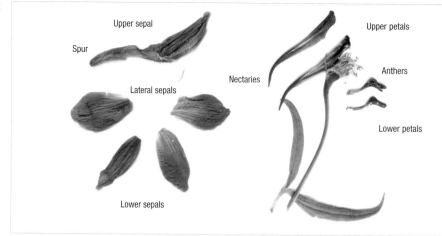

LEFT: **Figure 1.2a.**
The components of a flower of *D. elatum*, showing the characteristic sepal spur and nectaries.

known as an umbo on the back of the sepals is a fairly common feature of wild delphinium flowers.

You can see all the important flower components typical of a true delphinium by pulling to pieces a flower of *Delphinium elatum*, the species that is the principal ancestor of most garden delphiniums (see **Figure 1.2a**). The flower has five brightly coloured sepals, the uppermost having a hollow spur that projects behind the flower. This spur is often divided, with two points at the tip. Four petals form the eye of the flower. The two upper petals have rigid spurs that extend rearwards, each with a short tubular section that forms a nectary at the tip, and these fit inside the sepal spur. The left- and right-hand upper petals are distinguishable – one is the mirror image of the other – and their spurs fit closely together to form a tube that provides access to the nectaries. The two lower petals have no spur and broaden into a coloured blade, often covered with a beard of long hairs. These lower petals, sometimes called 'honey leaves', usually shield the numerous stamens and the three or more immature carpels (seedpods), which each terminate in a stigma.

The nectaries contain a sweet liquid that attracts bumblebees, other insect pollinators and hummingbirds to the flowers. The production of seed results from fertilization of the ovules (contained within the carpels) by pollen grains deposited on the stigma by such visitors. The seed combines the genetic information contained in the chromosomes of both ovule and pollen parent to produce the new delphinium that develops when the seed germinates. Wild delphiniums possess two sets of chromosomes in their cell nuclei, and are thus said to be diploid; in delphiniums, each set contains eight chromosomes. Each parent contributes only one set to the offspring. Naturally occurring mutations may increase the number of chromosome sets in a flower to four, making the plants tetraploid. The number of chromosomes can also be altered artificially by treating the plant with chemicals such as colchicine.

It is also worth noting here that the annual larkspurs – familiar garden flowers – are distinguished from delphiniums and assigned to a separate genus, *Consolida*, because flowers of their true wild ancestors have only a single spurred upper petal and just one carpel (see **Figure 1.2b**).

LEFT: **Figure 1.2b.**
A wild annual larkspur, showing the single seedpod for each floret that is characteristic of the genus *Consolida*.

Stems and Blooms

True delphiniums are herbaceous plants with no permanent woody stems above ground. The plant either dies immediately after flowering, as for the few annual and biennial species, or the flowering stem is renewed annually, as for all the many perennial species. The stem is erect or ascending and often hollow, with leaves distributed alternately along the stem or grouped in a basal rosette. It may grow to a height varying from 5 centimetres to 200 centimetres or more (2 to 78 inches), depending on the species and environment. The leaf blade is usually palmate, deeply divided into five lobes.

The flowers of a delphinium typically form a terminal raceme or spike in which five to one hundred or more flowers are arranged in a spiral around the upper part of the stem (see **Figure 1.3**). Each flower is on a stalk (pedicel) with a leaf bract where it joins the stem and two leaflets (bracteoles) between the base and the flower. The form of the bloom for both wild and cultivated delphiniums depends on the length of the flower stalks. The pedicels may be very short, resulting in long, narrow blooms in which the flowers are held close to the stem. Alternatively, the pedicels can be longer – either of uniform length so that the bloom has a wide columnar form, or decreasing steadily in length towards the top of the stem, giving a tapered spire of flowers.

The flowers are not always arranged in a raceme. In some species, especially those with a dwarf growth habit, the stem is extensively branched with a few flowers terminating each branch, or the stem has flowers grouped in a cluster (corymb) at the top.

Roots

The characteristics of a delphinium plant under the soil are of vital importance, for two reasons. First, the root system enables the plant to take up water and nutrients from the soil so it can grow. Second, at least part of the root of a perennial species must survive from one year to the next in order for the plant to flower again, and is the region where buds for new stems develop. Understanding the nature of the root system is therefore helpful in relation to cultivation methods, while knowing how new stems arise from the root is essential in the procedure of taking cuttings for vegetative propagation.

Several different types of root system are found in wild delphiniums that enable the plants to survive in harsh environments through the times when they are dormant. In semi-desert regions for example, where summer temperatures can be extremely high, delphinium species may survive as a tuber, and the roots are renewed annually. In less harsh environments, a semi-permanent area of woody tissue attached to the root develops at the base of stems and is known as the 'crown' of the plant. New stems develop from buds on the crown, and part of the root system may also be

BELOW: **Figure 1.3.** A typical cultivated delphinium bearing a terminal raceme of semi-double florets, leaf bracts and bracteoles.

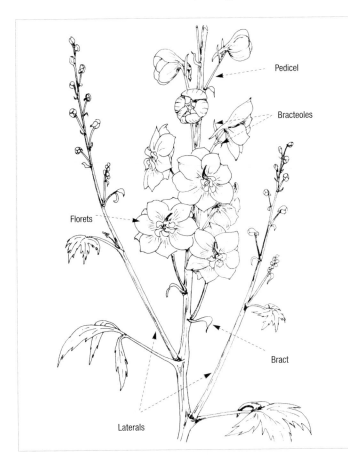

Pedicel

Bracteoles

Florets

Bract

Laterals

renewed annually. Other types of root structure with varying degrees of thickening of semi-permanent roots comparable to those of anemones, for example, are also found in wild delphiniums.

The root structure most relevant to cultivated delphiniums is that in which the plant has a permanent woody crown attached to a system of fibrous roots (see **Figure 1.4**). The drawing shows the features typical of a cultivated delphinium root after three phases of flower stem growth (the first two or three years). The current season's flower stems grow from the basal region of old stems, of which only the decaying stumps remain. The basal region has enlarged with age, becoming a thick, woody shell that is normally hollow. The woody basal regions of all the old stems together constitute the crown. Dormant buds, or eyes, from which new flower stems could grow, are widely distributed over the surface of the crown. It is easy to see that the base of the stems is fragile, and that failure to support the flower stems adequately can result in damage to the crown.

Roots extending from the crown supply nutrients and water for growth of the plant. Two types can be distinguished. There are anchor roots, which are thick dark-brown roots extending deep into the soil (40 centimetres/16 inches or more) from the base of the oldest part of the crown. These old roots, surviving from the first year's growth, serve as anchors for the plant. They are crucial for survival of the plant during periods of drought or winter dormancy, when they supply water and nutrients from deep underground. Moving a mature plant always breaks the anchor roots, and they do not seem to regenerate. There are also thin, yellowish young roots, called feeder roots, which spread outwards

from the crown to beyond the canopy of the leaves (50 centimetres/20 inches or more) and are located mainly within the surface layers of the soil. These much-branched roots grow rapidly during the summer months from the existing roots and the younger regions of the crown, including the basal regions of the growing flower stems. The uptake of nutrients and water through them determines the vigour of the plant and the quality of the flowers. Unfavourable soil conditions, such as drought after flowering or waterlogging during autumn and winter, can result in almost total loss of the feeder roots, which must then regenerate during the following season.

BELOW: **Figure 1.4.** Root structure of a cultivated delphinium showing the crown with dormant buds, together with anchor and feeder roots.

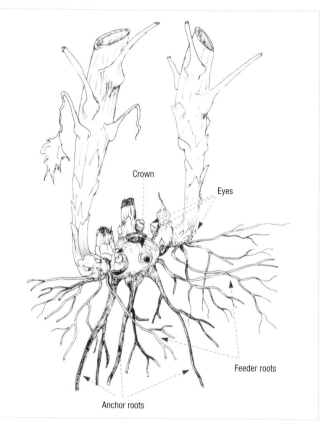

Crown

Eyes

Feeder roots

Anchor roots

2. A Survey of Wild Delphiniums

When choosing plants for our gardens, many of us have a strong tendency to surround ourselves with exotic flowers native to faraway places. In Britain, delphiniums belong in this category, as there are no delphiniums that are native to Britain in the wild. For hundreds of years, delphiniums have therefore been among the seeds and plants brought back by merchants and plant hunters from their travels. Nevertheless, it is very unlikely that the possibilities for bringing delphiniums with new features into cultivation have been exhausted. Growing a selection of wild delphiniums from around the world has taught us that there are many fascinating and beautiful features of their flowers for creative plant breeders to exploit if desired.

Where Delphiniums Grow

Delphiniums are plants of the northern hemisphere, except for a few species found south of the equator along the mountain ranges of Africa. Some three hundred or more distinct species are known and many of these have subspecies in different locations that can look very different from each other. They are found in climatic zones ranging from Arctic to tropical, but not in desert areas. The distribution of species is far from uniform, however, as seen in the diagram for Africa/Eurasia and North America (**Figure 2.1**). The areas of pronounced species diversity correspond to the high mountain ranges of central Asia and the mountains of western America. The greatest range of species – more than 60 – is found in Yunnan, a province of southern

BELOW: **Figure 2.1.** Distribution of *Delphinium* species in the northern hemisphere.

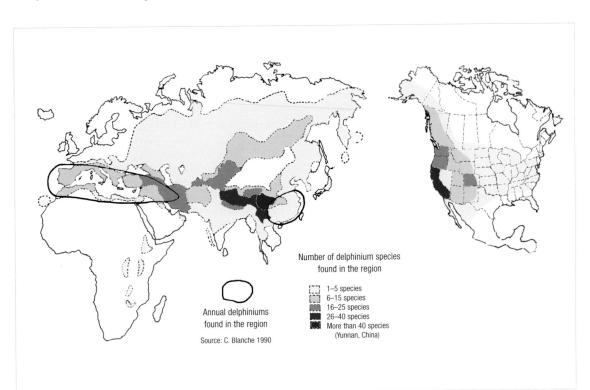

Number of delphinium species found in the region

Annual delphiniums found in the region

Source: C. Blanche 1990

1–5 species
6–15 species
16–25 species
26–40 species
More than 40 species
(Yunnan, China)

China, followed by the state of California in the US with 28.

The main factor responsible for so many distinct species is likely to be the rugged terrain of these areas, which allowed scattered populations of plants to evolve in isolation over many centuries. If delphinium species are removed from these isolated environments and grown in a garden, for example, they may hybridize with other delphinium species that flower at the same time. Hybrids are also seen in the wild if there is overlapping of the flowering times in areas where several species grow.

Most delphinium species are perennials, but a few are annuals or biennials. The three biennial species, *D. staphisagria*, *D. requienii* and *D. pictum*, are plants of the Mediterranean region, as are most of the 18 annual species. For example, *D. verdunense* is found in Spain and Portugal, *D. halteratum* is from France and Italy, and *D. peregrinum* is from Greece, Turkey and other countries of the eastern Mediterranean. The exception is *D. anthriscifolium*, an annual species found in low-altitude, temperate or sub-tropical regions of China.

Where Annual Larkspurs Grow

While the number of annual delphinium species is rather small, there are about 40 species of annual larkspurs in the genus *Consolida* that differ from delphiniums in having flowers with only a single spurred petal and one carpel. They occur throughout the temperate region where annual delphiniums are found, being distributed from the western end of the Mediterranean to Greece and Turkey, but also extending further northwards in Europe and eastwards into central Asia as far as Afghanistan. These larkspurs are plants of relatively low altitude, often being found as weeds in crops, or on stony slopes and in semi-desert regions.

The best-known annual larkspurs are *Consolida ambigua*, *C. orientalis* and *C. regalis*, as these are the principal ancestors of cultivated annual larkspurs. The distribution of purple-flowered *C. orientalis*

is particularly wide, extending from southern Spain to Azerbaijan and Iran, where it grows in vast masses. Other fascinating species include *C. camptocarpum* from Afghanistan, which has spikes of white or pale lilac-pink flowers, and *C. thirkeana* from the Kurdish region of Turkey and Iran, which in the Delphinium Society *Year Book* for 1966, Paul Furse says forms 'little bushy clumps dotted with pale mauve-and-white flowers'; it would be interesting to see them in cultivation.

Diversity in Delphinium Species

The most obvious differences between delphinium species are in the form and colour of their flowers. There may also be pronounced differences in the form of seedpods, and the fascinating variations in the size, shape and surface features of ripe seeds. Species vary greatly in plant architecture, some being tiny alpines with a bushy growth habit, while others are relative giants with thick stems, large leaves and long spikes of flowers. Species also differ in the extent to which stems, leaves and flowers are covered with hairs.

The form of leaves is a feature that clearly characterizes each species, and varies as a result of differences in the depth to which the leaf blade is dissected into lobes, the width of lobes and their further subdivision. The distribution of leaves also varies, since they may be regularly spaced on the stem up to the flowers, or almost entirely located at the base of the stem.

The nature of the root system is also variable, but unless a plant is dug out of the ground it is not immediately apparent if the flower stem is attached to a woody crown with fibrous roots or develops from a tuber. There are also large differences in the way the root system of a seedling develops, and the sensitivity of plants to disturbance or changes in environmental conditions. These differences influence the ease with which the plants may be cultivated.

This diversity of delphinium species has arisen as a result of adaptation of the plants to the varying environments where they grow, although the link is not always easy to

Wild Delphiniums: Diversity in Seeds

When you breed cultivated delphiniums, you quickly appreciate that the seeds of each cultivar are just as distinctive as the flowers. It can be their colour, size or shape that marks them out, so it comes as no surprise that seeds of wild delphiniums vary considerably between species.

A first obvious property is size. The largest delphinium seed we know is that of *D. staphisagria*, from Crete and the eastern Mediterranean (see **Figure 2.2a**). The seeds are almost the size of garden peas, being about 6 millimetres long by 5 millimetres wide (¼ by ³⁄₁₆ inch). The seedpods of *D. staphisagria* contain few seeds, and the plants are therefore not prolific seed producers. This is a rather surprising characteristic for a biennial plant that relies on seed distribution for its survival. However, the seeds have a tough, ridged coat and are well equipped to survive for long periods in the soil under the baking summer sunshine, even if it makes them difficult to germinate. In contrast, *D. requienii*, another of the Mediterranean biennial delphiniums, is a prolific producer of seeds that are only

about half as large, and germinate easily. These seeds have flat surfaces where they contact neighbouring seeds in the pod, and a curved surface where they touched the inner wall of the pod itself.

Annual delphiniums hailing from the Mediterranean region provide seeds at the other end of the size scale (see **Figure 2.2b**). The highly branched plants of *D. balcanicum*, for example, produce many very small seeds that repay a careful look at their features with a hand lens. They are almost spherical and about 1 millimetre (¹⁄₃₂ inch) in diameter but their surface looks rough due to a line of scales that winds in a spiral from bottom to top. A pit in the base often seems to have a hexagonal appearance, giving them the appearance of tiny socket-head screws.

Many delphinium species have seeds with scales covering their surface, but the prize for the most dramatic probably goes to those of the yellow-flowered *D. semibarbatum* (syn. *D. zalil*). These pale straw-coloured seeds look like miniature shuttlecocks (see **Figure 2.2c**).

D. semibarbatum shows that seeds do not need to be brown; quite a few wild delphiniums from California such as *D. variegatum* have seeds with a membranous outer coat that appears white (see **Figure 2.2d**). The seeds of other delphinium species have whitish ribs, but those of most species have a brown or black outer coat, and varying levels of surface roughness after ripening.

see. In the following sections we describe some of the distinctive characteristics that have fascinated us while growing a wide selection of delphinium species from seed.

BELOW FROM LEFT TO RIGHT: **Figure 2.2a.** The very large seeds of the biennial *D. staphisagria* have a tough, ridged coat.

Figure 2.2b. The tiny seeds of the annual *D. balcanicum* have basal pits.

Figure 2.2c. Scaly seeds of the yellow-flowered *D. semibarbatum* resemble miniature shuttlecocks.

Figure 2.2d. The membranous outer coat of seeds from *D. variegatum* gives them a strange appearance.

It is hard to guess the purpose of the surface features of seeds. They may be related to the mechanism of seed dispersal and thus influence survival of the species. Survival is also determined by the ability of seeds to withstand adverse weather conditions and to germinate once conditions become favourable. When you try to grow wild delphiniums from seed, it soon becomes apparent that there is a great deal of diversity between species with respect to the conditions required for germination. Because a high proportion of delphiniums originate in regions of alpine or continental climate, with severe winters, it is not surprising that seeds of many species germinate best at low temperature or require exposure to cold, moist conditions to initiate germination.

Wild Delphiniums: Diversity Below Ground

The roots of a delphinium anchor it in the ground and supply the water and nutrients required for growth. When these are the only functions of the root, as for annual delphiniums, it suffices for the plant to develop fibrous roots that die when the seed is ripe and the life cycle is complete. The top growth of perennial delphiniums is also renewed annually, but at least part of the root system must survive from year to year. Root survival depends greatly on climatic conditions, which determine how long it is dormant.

Many tall delphinium species from mountainous regions survive their period of winter dormancy by developing a woody area or 'crown' at the junction between the old flower stem and the roots. In many species, buds for new stems develop from the surface of the crown during the flowering season, and are present throughout the winter. In such cases, the main branches of the root system also survive. This is the situation for *D. elatum*, a plant from mountainous regions of Europe and further east. A similar permanent root system is found in many other Eurasian species and also in 17 American delphinium species, such as *D. glaucum*, a plant widely distributed throughout mountain ranges from Alaska south to Utah (see **Figure 2.3a**).

Climatic conditions that subject delphiniums to summer drought after they flower in spring require further adaptation of the root system. In *D. cardinale*, for example, the major roots become thickened; presumably they have a food-storage function. Buds for new stem growth are then not evident on the crown during the dormant period. In the usually moist soil conditions of an English summer, however, *D. cardinale* develops crown buds while flowering, and plants remain in almost continuous growth during autumn and winter, as do a number of other

FAR LEFT: **Figure 2.3a.** The roots of *D. glaucum*, showing a crown with two well-developed buds.

LEFT: **Figure 2.3b.** Thickened roots and developing crown buds of a plant of *D. cardinale* grown in the UK and lifted in autumn.

RIGHT: **Figure 2.3c.** Thickened storage roots of the Burmese species, *D. stapeliosmum.*

FAR RIGHT: **Figure 2.3d.** A tuber of *D. nuttallii*, with new fibrous roots and stem in early spring.

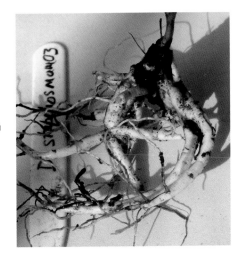

Californian delphinium species with a similar root structure (see **Figure 2.3b**). Examining the roots of *D. cardinale* indicates that most of the fibrous feeder roots are lost during dormancy, and are replaced when soil conditions become favourable. The new roots seem to grow from raised protrusions on the surface of the thickened roots.

Thickening of the roots so that they have a storage function is also seen in some Eurasian delphinium species. In Britain it is common to grow *D. tatsienense* as an annual, but we have found that older plants have a well-developed system of thickened roots. *D. stapeliosmum*, a pretty dwarf delphinium from Burma, also has thickened roots (see **Figure 2.3c**).

Many delphinium species from semi-desert regions have roots that are best described as tubers. This is the case for the yellow-flowered *D. semibarbatum* from Iran, Afghanistan and neighbouring countries. A tuberous root is also a normal feature of a large proportion of spring-flowering American delphinium species. Soil moisture and warmth at the end of winter stimulate the growth of new fibrous roots from the tuber, which is followed by development of a new stem, as in *D. nuttallii* (see **Figure 2.3d**). Such roots have no obvious buds for stem growth during the dormant period. We have been told that *D. tricorne* from the eastern

United States can be propagated by slicing root tubers into sections with 'eyes', from which stems will grow, in much the same way as potatoes.

Root structure influences the way delphiniums develop from seed. Root emergence is the first stage of seed germination, and it allows the seedling to take up water and nutrients from the soil. This is followed shortly afterwards by growth of a pair of seed leaves, which enable photosynthesis to start.

For delphinium species with fibrous root systems, branching of the root starts soon after seed germination. Swelling of the stem at the joint between the root and the cotyledon stalks perhaps corresponds to the first stage in development of a 'crown' from which the first true leaves grow. In American species that have tuberous roots, for example *D. nuttallianum*, seedling development is significantly different because a recognizable tuber develops (where the seed leaf stalk joins the root) before any true leaves appear. If weather conditions are then unsuitable, even at such an early stage, seedlings may stop developing and remain dormant until the following year before new roots and the first true leaves grow from the little tubers. This shows very clearly the importance of tuber formation for survival of these delphinium species through long periods of summer drought.

Wild Delphiniums: Diversity in Leaves

Delphiniums seen in the wild tend to be mature plants, but growing species from seed provides an opportunity to see how the foliage of the juvenile plant develops. Even here there are surprisingly large differences between species, so we look first at the leaves of seedlings.

Soon after the root emerges from a germinating delphinium seed, a pair of green seed leaves (cotyledons) appears and photosynthesis commences. At this stage, seedlings of most delphinium species have a pair of pointed oval seed leaves with distinct stalks attached to the root, and forming a 'V', as seen in a Californian species, *D. parishii* (**Figure 2.4a**). Cotyledons are characteristic of the species and it is no surprise to find that the very large seeds of *D. staphisagria* produce the largest cotyledons that grow to 30 millimetres long by 10 millimetres broad (1⅜ by ¼ inch; see **Figure 2.4b**). The leaf stalks for this species are relatively short when compared to those of *D. parishii*. The cotyledons can vary in shape from round (*D. vestitum*) to long and narrow (*D. uliginosum*), or may be covered with long hairs (*D. maackianum*).

When the cotyledons have individual stalks, the first true leaves grow from the junction between the cotyledon stalks and the root. There is, however, a quite different pattern of seedling development in a large group of American species that have tuberous roots, including red-flowered *D. nudicaule* from the west coast, *D. nuttallianum* from the Rocky Mountain states (see **Figure 2.4c**), and *D. tricorne* from the eastern states. In these species, the seed leaves grow from the top of a single stalk joined to the root (where a small root tuber develops) and form a 'T' or sometimes a 'Y'. The first true leaves grow from the tuber, which is generally hidden below the soil surface.

The mature leaf form typical of many tall wild delphiniums corresponds to the palmate leaves of *D. elatum* (see **Figure 2.5a**), which are quite deeply dissected

LEFT: **Figure 2.4a.** The cotyledons (seed leaves) of *D. parishii* arise on distinct stalks, forming a V-shape.

LEFT: **Figure 2.4b.** The dramatic, veined, 'giant' cotyledons of *D. staphisagria* are borne on relatively short stalks.

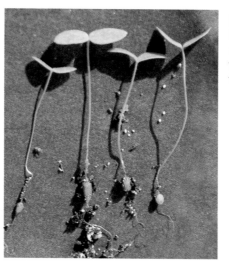

LEFT: **Figure 2.4c.** Cotyledons of *D. nuttallianum* arising from the top of a single stalk form a T-shape.

Figure 2.5. Leaves of wild delphiniums exhibit great diversity of form.

RIGHT: **Figure 2.5a.** *D. elatum.*

FAR RIGHT: **Figure 2.5b.** *D. vestitum.*

RIGHT: **Figure 2.5c.** *D. bulleyanum.*

FAR RIGHT: **Figure 2.5d.** *D. trolliifolium.*

towards the base. The leaves of *D. vestitum*, which comes from the Himalayan region, are strikingly different, since the shallow dissections create rounded lobes with a finely toothed margin (see **Figure 2.5b**). The growth habit of the plant also differs from that of *D. elatum*, with a basal cluster of very large leaves on hairy stalks 30 centimetres (12 inches) tall developing before the flower stem starts to grow. The dwarf Himalayan species *D. brunonianum* and *D. cashmerianum* also have leaves with broad lobes and a toothed margin. Deeply dissected leaves with rather narrow lobes, like that in **Figure 2.5c**, are characteristic of many species. The leaves of this plant (of uncertain identity – possibly *D. bulleyanum*) are patterned with pale spots at the base of each leaf division. This feature, which adds interest to the appearance of the foliage, might be considered a questionable virtue when you realize that such leaves look remarkably like those of common buttercups. It is rather easy to mistake one for the other when weeding a border!

While it might seem unforgivable to mistake a precious delphinium for a weed, the similarity of the leaf to that of a plant of another genus has sometimes been used as the basis for naming newly discovered delphiniums. One example is *D. trolliifolium*, found in the Columbia River Gorge region and other parts of Oregon in the United States (see **Figure 2.5d**), presumably given this name because the leaves closely resemble those of the Globeflower, *Trollius europaeus*. Two other delphinium found in the Columbia River

Gorge region are *D. nuttallii* (**Figure 2.5e**), and *D.* x *burkei* (**Figure 2.5f**). Although these three delphiniums all have dissected leaves, their appearance is so distinctive that the leaves can be used to identify any self-sown seedlings that appear in a garden border where all three species are growing together.

Leaves of *D. balcanicum*, an annual species from Greece, are unusual for a delphinium because the leaf blade tapers into the stalk (see **Figure 2.5g**). Another annual species, *D. venulosum*, has leaves of similar 'cuneate' form but perhaps the most striking example is *D. uliginosum*, a dwarf perennial delphinium from southern California with greyish leaves bearing a considerable resemblance to fish forks!

In many delphiniums, dissection of the leaf blade into narrow lobes is far more extreme than in the species mentioned so far. For example, leaves of the dwarf species *D. tatsienense* (**Figure 2.5i**) are divided into quite narrow lobes, while those of *D. semibarbatum* (**Figure 2.5h**) are dissected into long slender ribbons. The lacy foliage of this yellow-flowered delphinium from semi-desert regions withers when the plant is in flower.

The shape of lobes or undulations of their surface are not the only factors that influence the appearance of delphinium leaves. If hairs are present at the leaf margin or on either the upper or lower surfaces, these affect the way leaves reflect light. For example, the dwarf species *D. ceratophorum*, from the highlands of Yunnan, has leaves covered with white hairs (see **Figure 2.5j**), which look grey if you look at them from a certain angle. The leaves of *D. caucasicum* (**Figure 2.5k**) are also covered with hairs, and at times they appear white, as if covered with mildew. From a gardener's point of view it is unfortunate that hairy leaves seem to be very favourable sites for the development of mildew. For mildew-resistant delphiniums we should therefore look out for species with smooth, waxy leaves. One that matches this description is *D. requienii*, which has large, fleshy leaves that shine in the sun.

From the delphinium leaves that have been considered so far, it might be thought that the leaf blade is always regularly divided into lobes, uniformly decorated with hairs or neatly patterned with pale spots at the base of the lobe divisions. The young leaves of *D. hansenii*, however, rather spoil this pattern by being covered irregularly with curious chocolate blotches (that on first glance appear to be diseased) but that disappear as the leaves grow (see **Figure 2.5l**).

ABOVE: **Figure 2.5e.** *D. nuttallii.*

ABOVE: **Figure 2.5f.** *D.x burkei.*

RIGHT: **Figure 2.5g.**
D. balcanicum.

FAR RIGHT: **Figure 2.5h.**
D. semibarbatum.

RIGHT: **Figure 2.5i.**
D. tatsienense.

FAR RIGHT: **Figure 2.5j.**
D. ceratophorum.

RIGHT: **Figure 2.5k.**
D. caucasicum.

FAR RIGHT: **Figure 2.5l.**
D. hansenii.

Wild Delphiniums: Diversity in Flowers

The primary justification for our interest in wild delphiniums is their flowers, because they show the range of form and colour that might be found one day in garden flowers. The selection of species here is not truly representative, as it includes only delphiniums that we have grown from seed. Our knowledge of the species is also incomplete in the sense that we have not seen them in their natural setting. A delphinium grown in a flower border or pot can look very different from a plant of the same species on a mountainside or in a woodland glade, whether that is in California or Kashmir.

In this survey we look first at some delphiniums from the Mediterranean region and then move eastwards towards the Himalayan mountains and northwards to Siberia.

The biennial species *D. staphisagria*, from Crete, is an interesting plant to grow because it was one of the first delphiniums to be described in historical records, and is often the first species mentioned in accounts of the genus. The plant is similar in some respects to familiar border delphiniums, having rather smooth palmate leaves, a widely spaced, tapered flower spike and strong side shoots. The individual flowers, however, are distinctly unusual. The spur that is supposedly the signature of delphiniums is just a knob on the back of the upper sepal and it seems too short to accommodate the petal spurs. The

development of colour in the flower is also curious. Sepals and petals are greeny-yellow when buds open, with just faint indications of violet-purple colour around sepal edges and in veins. The colour develops as the flower ages, but remains attractively patterned in both sepals and petals, while prominent brown anthers add interest to the eye (see **Figure 2.6a**). Swelling of the exceptionally fat seedpods makes a grand finale to the fascinating flower display.

The flowers of *D. requienii*, another of the biennial species that come from the Mediterranean region, are of similar form to those of *D. staphisagria*, although they have a short but distinct spur. The quite small florets are a fascinating mixture of pale lavender with pinkish tinges. Although blooms are rather muted in colouring, *D. requienii* is amazingly floriferous and makes an interesting feature in a garden.

Staying with short-lived delphiniums, *D. balcanicum* from Greece and adjacent countries of the Balkans, is an annual. Plants of this species with a branching growth habit reached 1 metre (39 inches) tall when grown in fertile soil and were covered with 10 centimetre- (4 inch-) long spikes of small dark-blue flowers (**Figure 2.6b**). Tiny self-sown plants that appeared in subsequent years growing in cracks between paving had just a few pretty clusters of blue flowers, and are perhaps more typical of how these plants might appear on a sun-baked hillside.

Mountainous regions to the north and east of the Balkans are the home of *D. elatum*, which grows up to 2 metres

Figure 2.6. Flowers of wild delphinium species from Europe and Asia.

FAR LEFT: **Figure 2.6a.** *D. staphisagria.*

LEFT: **Figure 2.6b.** *D. balcanicum.*

RIGHT: **Figure 2.6c.**
D. elatum.

RIGHT: **Figure 2.6d.**
D. speciosum.

RIGHT: **Figure 2.6e.**
D. speciosum.

RIGHT: **Figure 2.6f.**
D. vestitum.

(78 inches) tall in sparse woodland or among tall vegetation in meadows and in river valleys. It is interesting to grow this ancestor of cultivated tall delphiniums, which has spikes of flowers at the top of upright stems. We started from seed derived from *D. elatum* collected in the Tatra Mountains of Slovakia. However, some seedlings we raised had flowers with white eyes, which suggests they might be hybrids. Other seedlings had flowers of the type expected for *D. elatum*, with deep blue or bluish-violet sepals 15–20 millimetres (⅝–¾ inch) in length, dark brown petals in the eye and a spur longer than the sepals (see **Figure 2.6c**).

While there are other delphinium species rather like *D. elatum* from eastern Europe and western Asia, *D. caucasicum* and *D. speciosum* from the Caucasus Mountains are quite different in habit and in the form of their flowers. *D. caucasicum* is a plant of glacial moraines in the alpine zone, with sturdy hairy stems, mainly basal leaves and large violet-blue flowers. *D. speciosum* is a taller plant of sub-alpine meadows, but is also hairy, and the ones we raised also had violet-blue flowers. An impressive feature of the plants when grown in the garden is that the base of their blooms is so close to the ground. We would be really excited if we could achieve such a short stem below the flowers in the delphinium cultivars that we breed. A fascinating feature of the blooms and the individual florets is that their appearance reminds us strongly of bellflowers (see **Figure 2.6d**). The flared tips of sepals make the florets truly bell-shaped when the buds first open. The long upper petals (**Figure 2.6e**) also allow you to imagine that the dark brown eyes have the profile of a rabbit rather than a bee!

D. vestitum, from the mountains of northern India and Kashmir, is another species with leaves mainly in a basal cluster. The large, almost undivided leaves have been mentioned previously, but the goblet-shaped violet flowers are also interesting, with the black petals of the eye being split into two lobes at the tip. The flowers, like the rest of the plant, are covered with long hairs (see **Figure 2.6f**).

Staying with violet-blue flowers, *D. brunonianum* and *D. cashmerianum*, from high altitudes in the Himalaya, have flowers that seem designed to protect the pollen-bearing anthers and stigmas from strong wind and the monsoon rain. Instead of being spread out along an upright spike, the flowers cluster together at the top of a short stem and tend to look downwards. The florets have unusual, inflated spurs, giving the florets a rather globular appearance, especially for *D. brunonianum* (see **Figure 2.6g**). The petals of both species should be black or dark brown, but those of some plants we have grown were pale brown.

Possibly the most spectacular delphinium of central Asia – and an exciting, if challenging, plant to grow in the garden – is the yellow-flowered beauty, *D. semibarbatum*, which is a plant of semi-desert slopes in the foothills north of the great mountain ranges of Iran and Afghanistan. The loosely spaced spikes of flowers terminate every wiry stem of the highly branched plants. The wide-opening florets, with broad flat sepals, can be up to 25–30 millimetres (1–1³⁄₁₆ inches) in diameter. Their colour varies from pale primrose to stronger yellows, with flecks of orange on the tips of the upper petals in the eye (see **Figure 2.6h**).

D. stapeliosmum is an elegant dwarf delphinium from the eastern end of the Himalayan ranges in Burma, and has luminous purple flowers borne in small numbers on each shoot of a thin but tough branched stem. The flower has a very slender long spur, and the broad upper sepal has a sharp point at the tip associated with a prominent green umbo on the outer surface (see **Figure 2.6i**). Plants of *D. stapeliosmum*, like *D. semibarbatum*, have a thickened or tuberous root.

Tough, branched stems are also a feature of *D. ceratophorum*, which comes from high-altitude regions of Yunnan close to Tibet. Stem branching seems to be triggered by flower-bud formation at the tip of a shoot, as each time a flower cluster develops, a new stem appears at the last leaf joint and the process repeats, resulting in a

TOP: **Figure 2.6g.** *D. brunonianum.*

MIDDLE: **Figure 2.6h.** *D. semibarbatum.*

BOTTOM: **Figure 2.6i.** *D. stapeliosmum.*

prostrate rather than upright growth habit. The flowers have broad bluish-violet sepals with mauve tinges, and their spur curves strongly downwards at the tip. The upper petals have deep blue tips while the lower two have a dark basal region with a beard of yellowish hairs and paler violet-blue blades (see **Figure 2.6j**).

A notable feature of the flower of *D. bulleyanum* is its spur, which curves downwards and coils. This attractive and very floriferous plant from China has upright branching stems, and spikes of widely spaced flowers on every shoot. The small florets, 20 millimetres (¾ inch) in diameter, are purple-blue and have dark eye petals with beards of yellow hairs (see **Figure 2.6k**). It seems unlikely that the spurs are meant to serve the same function as tendrils on a climbing plant, but they certainly lead to the flowers becoming impossibly entangled after a gale, or when you try to cut some for a vase.

Moving further north, the Pacific coast region of Russia close to Vladivostok is the home of *D. maackianum*, a delphinium growing to about 1 metre (39 inches) tall that is in many respects similar to *D. elatum*. The deep-crimson flower stems and their side shoots have loosely packed, tapering spikes of dark-blue flowers with long straight spurs (see **Figure 2.6m**). The most fascinating feature of the plant, however, is not the flowers but the exceptionally large, deep-crimson leaf bracts at the base of each flower stalk. The effect of these bracts as the blooms begin to expand is remarkable, and creates a plant that looks rather like a salvia.

The diligence of a few wildflower seed collectors and friends in the United States opened our eyes to the world of North American delphiniums, which perhaps first arrived there by spreading from Siberia across the Bering Strait to Alaska. Indeed, *D. brachycentrum*, the so-called Arctic larkspur, occurs both in northern Siberia and Alaska, where it grows on well-drained tundra slopes. But we start our North American survey with plants of the eastern states – where only a few species are found – and work westward to delphinium heaven

TOP: **Figure 2.6j.** *D. ceratophorum.*

MIDDLE: **Figure 2.6k.** *D. bulleyanum.*

BOTTOM: **Figure 2.6m.** *D. maackianum.*

in California. It is worth noting that the wild delphiniums of North America are commonly called larkspurs.

D. exaltatum, which is found along the Appalachian Mountains from Pennsylvania southwards, grows up to 2 metres (78 inches) tall on rocky slopes in open woodland. The smooth leaves and narrow, columnar bloom of purple-tinged flowers remind us of the biennial *D. requienii* rather than *D. elatum*, but our plants proved perennial, both when grown in pots and in the border.

The most frequently encountered wild delphinium of the eastern states is said to be *D. tricorne*, a dwarf tuberous-rooted species with short tapered spikes of quite large flowers, and growing to a height of about 30 centimetres (12 inches). The colour range includes violet-blues, purple, lavender and pure white (see **Figure 2.7a**). We have read reports of *D. tricorne* being grown successfully in a Massachusetts garden. However, it would be hard to make any extensive planting of this delphinium in Britain because it is particularly difficult to raise from seed.

From further west comes the 'Plains Larkspur', *D. carolinianum*, subsp. *virescens*, which has white flowers with long spurs that point skywards (see **Figure 2.7b**). Plants flower in the first year from seed. In our experience so far, few survive to a second year, perhaps because the roots resent being wet during the winter. Other

sub-species of *D. carolinianum* from the southern states have blue or purple flowers.

Another species with white flowers, *D. wootonii* (formerly called *D. virescens*, subsp. *wootonii*) is found in the south-west, in New Mexico and adjacent states. The flowers are notable for the fascinating beards of long white hairs on the petals.

Three species that were introduced to us from the Columbia River Gorge region close to the Pacific coast of Oregon are worthy of note. The first to note is *D. nuttallianum* because this has a wide distribution over the western United States and Canada, where it generally grows in well drained, open woodland or grassy areas. It was exciting to see the flowers of this tuberous-rooted dwarf delphinium because the dainty little plants had taken three years from seed to reach flowering size. The violet veining of the petals and reflexed lateral sepals are notable features of the flowers (see **Figure 2.7c**).

RIGHT: **Figure 2.7d.**
D. leucophaeum.

FAR RIGHT: **Figure 2.7f.**
*D. orfordii (*syn.
D. decorum).

For garden use, *D. trolliifolium* is the best delphinium from the Columbia River Gorge that we grow. Seedlings normally flower in their second year, and when mature are sturdy plants with loosely spaced, tapered blooms up to 1.4 metres (55 inches) tall in spring, several weeks earlier than *elatum* group delphiniums. The quite large flowers are generally bright blue in colour, and the white tips of the upper petals provide a nice contrast. The colour can range from dark violet blue to paler lavender shades.

D. nuttallii also flowers in the second year from seed and persists in the open ground, but it is a much smaller plant that grows only 30–50 centimetres (12–20 inches) tall. The neat spikes of small blue or purple florets are attractive, and the upper petals of both forms have bright blue tips.

The persistence of the bright blue upper petals in colour variants of *D. nuttallii* is interesting in relation to *D. leucophaeum* from the central Willamette valley of Oregon, which is listed as *D. nuttallii,* subsp. *ochroleucum* in the *Flora of North America*. This delphinium resembles *D. nuttallii* in most respects, but is quite remarkable in having white or yellowish sepals set off by the blue-tipped upper petals (see **Figure 2.7d**). A white delphinium with a blue eye turns on its head the commonly held belief that delphiniums should all have blue flowers with a white eye. Plant breeders sometimes

spend their whole lives trying to achieve such a transformation.

The west coast provides several other delphiniums with flowers in dramatic eye-catching colours. One of them that has been cultivated for at least a hundred years is *D. nudicaule*, a short-growing species with fiery orange-red flowers, which grows in moist sites in southern Oregon and the coastal regions of California (see **Figure 2.7e**). In Britain this species can survive for several years in the open ground. In our garden it flowers later than in the Coast Mountains of California, where it is the earliest delphinium and can be in flower by Easter. Growing this species from the seed of wild plants is interesting, since the plants often have longer tapering spikes of flowers than dwarf commercial selections.

Another spring-flowering dwarf species from meadows in the northern Coast Range of California is *D. decorum*. We have grown plants from seed distributed as *D. orfordii* (syn. *D. decorum?*) that made ideal pot plants with many large flowers, of similar character and colour range to the flowers of *D. trolliifolium* (see **Figure 2.7f**).

FAR RIGHT: **Figure 2.7e.**
D. nudicaule.

FAR LEFT: **Figure 2.7g.**
D. variegatum.

LEFT: **Figure 2.7h.**
D. gypsophilum.

FAR LEFT: **Figure 2.7i.**
D. hesperium subsp.
pallescens.

LEFT: **Figure 2.7j.**
D. amabile.

FAR LEFT: **Figure 2.7k.**
D. cardinale.

LEFT: **Figure 2.7m.**
D. californicum subsp.
interius.

The so-called Swamp Larkspur, *D. uliginosum*, which originates in streamside and grassland sites in northern California, provides flowers of a different style, with up-turned spurs. The almost leafless slender stems rise from a basal rosette of curious leaves that wither at flowering time in late spring or early summer.

D. variegatum, the Royal Larkspur, is a widely distributed dwarf delphinium of grassland and open oak woods in California. It flowers a little later in spring than *D. nudicaule*, before being baked dry during the long, hot and rainless summer. When this plant is grown in pots the very large, wide-open blue or purple-blue flowers of such tiny plants are very rewarding and have some lovely qualities that would make them highly desirable as dwarf delphiniums for garden use (see **Figure 2.7g**).

The cooler and moister conditions in Britain make it possible to have other, taller Californian delphiniums flowering in summer from sowings in late winter. The pastel blue and pinkish lilac flowers of *D. recurvatum*, the Valley Larkspur, and the pink-tinged white flowers of *D. gypsophilum* (**Figure 2.7h**), are delightful. The structure of the tall plants of species such as *D. hesperium*, subsp. *pallescens* (**Figure 2.7i**), with many flowers distributed along long slender wiry stems, is an interesting contrast to the heavy foliage and blooms of our border delphiniums. While these species prove straightforward to grow from seed, several other species resent root disturbance but, with care and some luck, you can also enjoy the pale blue flowers of *D. amabile* (**Figure 2.7j**), or the white flowers of *D. parishii* subsp. *pallidium*, on slender wiry stems.

Delphinium cardinale, the Scarlet Larkspur, hails from southern California and is a tall-growing delphinium with stems that branch extensively to prolong the spectacular display of scarlet flowers in loosely packed spikes. The regularly spaced florets open wider than those of *D. nudicaule* to reveal their long, yellow-tipped upper petals (see **Figure 2.7k**). An interesting aspect of *D. cardinale* is that

there are variants to tempt plant breeders with yellow flowers, and also fully double flowers. We have found that in well-drained sites plants of this species survive for several years, but winter losses can be high for plants grown in heavy soil.

D. californicum subsp. *interius*, the Hospital Canyon larkspur from the west coast of California, is a delphinium with fibrous roots that grows well in the open ground and produces long spikes with large numbers of very small flowers held close to the stem. The flowers remain cupped, but their greeny-yellow colouring and the pink-tinged upper petals are fascinating (see **Figure 2.7m**).

The Poisonous Properties of Delphiniums

While delphiniums are greatly valued for the beauty of their flowers, we must not forget that humans first became interested in them as a source of medicines. This use implies that delphiniums contain substances with significant biological activity that can potentially be toxic to man and other animals, so they need to be treated with some caution as 'potentially poisonous' plants. It is now common practice for delphinium plants, and packets of delphinium seeds, to be labelled with a warning to the effect that 'plant material or seeds may prove harmful if eaten'.

The biologically active substances in delphiniums can interfere with the human nervous system, which is why, in carefully controlled doses, they have been used in herbal medicine since ancient times for pain relief, and as sedatives, emetics and love potions. For thousands of years, crushed delphinium seed was also used as an insecticide to kill body lice.

The downside to the presence of toxic substances in delphiniums is that sometimes they may have seriously harmful effects on animals that eat large quantities of plant material. In the United States, grazing of wild delphiniums in spring causes cattle poisoning, especially in the western foothills of the Rocky Mountains.

Wild delphiniums there have the status of noxious weeds, which has led to the use of herbicide sprays to control them. The situation is comparable to that in the UK with ragwort, a noxious weed that can be fatal for horses, and which landowners are required by law to control.

The potential for medicinal use of chemicals that could be extracted from delphiniums has stimulated many scientific studies of their chemical make-up. These show that the toxic chemicals are diterpenoid alkaloids, which are also found in the more highly toxic plants of the genus *Aconitum*. An astonishing variety of these chemicals are found in wild delphiniums, with more than 150 different alkaloids having been identified. The studies show that even in this respect, delphinium species differ from one another, with variation in both the number and molecular structure of the alkaloids. For example, one study found 16 different alkaloids in *D. montanum*, a delphinium from the Pyrenees, but only 9 from the annual species *D. gracile*. Some of the alkaloids were compounds that are also found in the American delphinium species *D. cardinale* and *D. nudicaule*. It is interesting to note that the names given to many of the alkaloids relate to the delphinium species from which they were first isolated, for example *bicolor*idine, *elat*ine, *nudicaul*-idine, and *peregrin*idine.

The studies of delphinium toxicity made in relation to cattle poisoning showed that the toxicity of plant material varies substantially between species. It was found, for example, that extracts from *D. barbeyi* were about ten times more toxic than material from a cultivated garden delphinium; toxicity was also greatest in plants making rapid growth. The differences in toxicity between delphinium species evidently reflect the particular alkaloids present in a species, since some of the alkaloids are up to 100 times more potent as neuromuscular poisons than others.

It is evident from the chemical studies that all delphiniums contain potent toxins. However, this is not an unfamiliar situation in our gardens, as many familiar plants – for example aconitums and foxgloves – are equally or more poisonous. At some stage in our childhood we have to learn not to put such plant material in our mouths. Obviously, it is essential that all adults and parents need to get the message across to children that 'delphiniums are poisonous', although without making them unduly alarmed. It would be nice to hope that one day we could tell them that delphiniums are the original source of a wonder drug, like the heart stimulant Digoxin, which is obtained from foxgloves.

An interesting question is why delphiniums should contain alkaloids in the first place, but none of the answers is very convincing. One suggestion is that they provide a defence mechanism against grazing animals by giving the plant an unpleasant taste. That does not seem plausible when you see the massive damage that small mammals like voles can do to young shoots and the crowns of cultivated delphiniums. Slugs and snails are certainly not deterred from eating the plants. Another possibility is that the chemicals act as anti-feedants for insect pests. In Britain, cultivated delphiniums are not normally subject to severe aphid infestation but this is not true in the United States, where they can be heavily infected by Rosy Aphis. We find that many wild delphiniums are prone to attack by a variety of insects and show no sign of having any natural protection.

3. Delphiniums in Cultivation

Over the years plant suppliers have, in response to customer preferences, introduced many improved or novel types of delphinium with larger flowers, new colours and shorter or more branched stems. The relationship of modern cultivated delphiniums to their wild ancestors is usually either poorly documented or wrongly interpreted, so rather than add to the confusion, we prefer to concentrate on cultivated delphiniums as they are today.

It is convenient to start by dividing garden delphiniums into four groups.

- **Elatum Group:** These have an upright hollow stem with broad-lobed leaves clothing the lower part and many flowers spirally arranged along the upper part to form a prominent primary bloom. They are similar in form to, and are probably derived from, *Delphinium elatum*, a native plant of the European Alps and mountain ranges further east, although their development may have involved hybridization with some other species.
- **Belladonna Group:** These have extensive branching at leaf joints resulting in stems with a small terminal bloom, and strong side-shoots with terminal blooms. The leaves are generally extensively dissected with narrow lobes. When first introduced, Belladonna cultivars all had a similar origin and differed in their genetic characteristics from *elatum* hybrids. The name is now widely used (and sometimes misused) to describe delphiniums of various origins.
- **Grandiflorum Group:** These are dwarf delphiniums that have small terminal clusters of flowers on branched stems with highly dissected leaves. The Asiatic species *Delphinium grandiflorum* and its variants are important ancestors of this appealing group.
- **Species, and Species Hybrids:** Some wild delphiniums are found in cultivation, but forms available in commerce are often selections with improved flowers and better habit.

Elatum Group

Modern cultivated delphiniums have much larger flowers, in a far wider range of colours, than their wild ancestors. This situation has been reached through the continual selection of plants showing improvements relative to those currently available. At some stage this process resulted in selection of plants with double the basic number of chromosomes for a delphinium, a characteristic that is often associated with increased vigour and flower size. As a result, Elatum-group delphiniums are genetically tetraploids (having four sets of chromosomes) rather than diploid (two sets). This leads to complications when attempts are made to introduce new characteristics or colours from other diploid delphinium species, as will be seen in relation to Belladonna delphiniums and the breeding of delphiniums with red flowers.

The most important characteristics of Elatum-group delphinium cultivars are the form and colour of the flowers. It is convenient to distinguish three types of flower, differing in the number of sepals, petals and carpels present, although flowers of intermediate type are quite common (see **Figure 3.1**). Flowers with just five sepals, as in a wild delphinium, are said to be single. When the flower has a second layer of eight sepals and the petals form a distinct eye, it is described as semi-double. When further layers of sepals are present and the distinction between sepals and petals is lost so that there is no distinct eye, the flower is said to be double.

In Britain and North America, single flowers in Elatum cultivars are generally

Figure 3.1. Types of flower form for Elatum-group cultivars:

LEFT: **Figure 3.1a.** Single flowers with 5 sepals.

FAR LEFT: **Figure 3.1b.** Semi-double flowers with 13 sepals.

LEFT: **Figure 3.1c.** Double flowers with more than 13 sepals.

regarded as a serious fault, because they are normally associated with rapid seed set and flowers that start dropping to pieces before buds near the top of the bloom begin to open. In continental Europe, cultivars with single flowers remain popular, especially if the colour is a beautifully clear blue.

Delphiniums with fully double flowers remain uncommon and the majority of top-class cultivars have semi-double flowers. The flower of one of the finest named Elatum cultivars, 'Gordon Forsyth' (**Figure 3.1b**), illustrates well the improvements in flower quality compared to wild *D. elatum*.

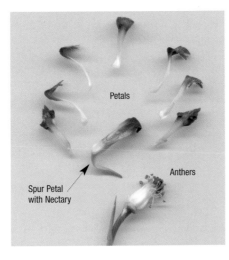

ABOVE: **Figure 3.2.** The multiple petals of **'Gordon Forsyth'** displayed to show one single-spurred petal with a nectary.

Petals

Anthers

Spur Petal with Nectary

The sepals open wide to form an almost flat disc of colour 80 millimetres (3 inches) or more in diameter. The eye also contains extra petals in a tight cluster of contrasting colour so that it is a prominent feature of the flower. The blooms of this cultivar can have 50 or more flowers regularly positioned along a stem 100–130 centimetres (39–51 inches) long.

Surprisingly for a delphinium, the flower of 'Gordon Forsyth' usually has only a single spurred petal with a nectary that is exposed in the face of the flower rather than hidden inside the sepal spur (see **Figure 3.2**). This spurred petal differs in structure from the nectaries of wild *D. elatum*.

A feature of Elatum cultivars is the expanded range of flower colour compared to the restricted range of purple-blue shades found in *D. elatum*. There are now cultivars with flowers in white, creamy white, pink shades (usually with a bluish tinge), lavender, violets, purples and blues varying from soft pastel shades to intense royal blue. Even delphiniums with flowers in dark brown or black shades can be obtained. The colour is not necessarily uniform but may be interestingly patterned to produce, for example, sepals having

either a central band or edges of a different colour. The appearance of the flowers is further enhanced by the colour of the eye, which can be white, black, shades of brown from pale fawn to dark chocolate, or even patterned with stripes or flecks of the sepal colour.

The use of species other than *D. elatum* in the later development of cultivated delphiniums is probably part of the reason for these extensions of the colour range. However, colours such as white, pink, violet and even black are associated with genetically recessive genes often present in *elatum* hybrids. Flowers in these colours can therefore be produced by careful selection of the parent plants used in breeding programmes, as discussed in chapter 4.

Elatum-group Delphiniums in Commerce

On the basis of the method used for propagation, two distinct classes of Elatum-group delphinium can be recognized. The first group comprises selected individual named cultivars; these can only be propagated vegetatively. The second group includes named selections that are propagated from seed.

The approach adopted during the past century by most nursery gardeners in Europe was to select individual plants raised in their breeding programmes with flowers of exceptional quality. These would then be assessed further for other desirable characteristics, such as resistance to disease and a reliably perennial growth habit. The best of the selected individuals were given names prior to their introduction. As such named cultivars do not breed true from seed, they must be propagated vegetatively to produce identical plants for distribution to customers. Traditionally this has required delphinium specialists to maintain for each named cultivar a large collection of stock plants from which cuttings are taken. It is now also possible to maintain stocks of named delphiniums as tissue cultures kept under laboratory conditions, with young plants being raised from them by micropropagation techniques, as described in chapter 7.

The second approach, which dominates the supply of delphiniums world-wide, is for plant breeders to supply Elatum-group delphiniums either as a named seed selection or as young plants raised from such a seed selection. The aim of the breeder is to supply seeds that yield plants with particular characteristics, such as a specific colour or plant height.

Named Delphinium Cultivars

The number of entries in the *International Register of Delphinium Names* is colossal, and there are many further cultivar names that are not registered. The bulk of these names relate to cultivars that are now extinct, or unavailable to most people, so our survey of named cultivars will cover a very limited selection that we regard as typical of modern delphiniums. The naming of delphiniums has been primarily associated with delphinium growers in Britain and, over the past 60 years, the source of new named cultivars has changed dramatically. In the early years of this period nurseries that specialized in herbaceous perennials and had significant delphinium-breeding programmes, such as Bakers or Blackmore & Langdon, introduced most new delphiniums. Unfavourable economic trends forced the closure or curtailed the activities of such nurseries, and by 1980 even Blackmore & Langdon had ceased breeding delphiniums. Since the mid-1970s most new introductions have come from amateur enthusiasts or small nurseries, with the cultivars that are selected for naming either coming from small-scale programmes of hand-crossing or being particularly attractive chance seedlings. Such cultivars are often difficult to obtain. The range of named cultivars currently available thus includes established ones at least 35 years old plus more recent introductions in a wider range of colours.

Named delphinium cultivars are not normally obtainable from garden centres, and must be obtained from delphinium specialists instead. This is because the number of rooted cuttings that can be produced of any particular cultivar is generally too small to justify distribution of the plants through the normal garden centre supply chain. However, there are signs that the situation is changing as more cultivars are held in tissue cultures, from which plantlets in small plugs can be produced in large quantities.

The fact that a delphinium has a name is no guarantee of quality, and the best way to assess the cultivar is to grow it. There is a limit to how many plants anyone can grow, so our assessments of most cultivars are based on seeing the flowers of plants grown by others. This can be done by visiting places where delphiniums are grown, such as gardens open to the public, a nursery specializing in delphiniums when their plants are in flower, or the Trial of Delphiniums, a long-term trial of new varieties being undertaken at the Royal Horticultural Society's Garden at Wisley. Other opportunities include the displays of delphiniums by nurserymen at horticultural shows – which are often useful venues because the plants can be purchased – and blooms exhibited by amateur growers in competitions at flower shows. When assessing the qualities of named cultivars that are new to us, we apply the criteria we use to evaluate seedlings from our own delphinium breeding. Those criteria, discussed in chapters 4 and 7, are in large measure based on looking carefully at named delphiniums and deciding which features of each flower appeal to us.

Named Delphiniums with White Flowers

Looking back, it appears that the development of delphiniums with white flowers in Britain was rather neglected, and left to amateur raisers. The 'Galahad' and 'Percival' seed-raised Pacific Hybrids series then arrived on the scene, providing white flowers of excellent quality. Ronald Parrett's book *Delphiniums* (1961) lists seven cultivars, the most famous being Frank Bishop's 'Swanlake', which provided very tall narrow spikes of white flowers with black eyes. 'Swanlake' and the short-growing 'Purity' (with a white eye) may survive in collections of historic varieties, but the others are now just distant memories.

ABOVE RIGHT: **Figure 3.3.** **'Olive Poppleton'** (AGM), with white florets, has a delightful honey-brown eye.

BELOW RIGHT: **Figure 3.4.** The clean white florets of **'Lilian Bassett'** (AGM) have a dramatic black eye.

The named white delphiniums of today have mostly been raised and introduced by amateur enthusiasts. The oldest still available is **'Rona'**, raised in 1964 by T O Cowan from white delphinium breeding lines of purely English origin. This is a fine, tall-growing delphinium still capable of producing long, broad blooms of large white flowers with white eyes. The flowers are of good substance, and last well as the bloom develops. Despite being less satisfactory in this respect, **'Olive Poppleton'** (which won the Award for Garden Merit – **AGM**) has also stood the test of time because the clean white florets have an attractive golden-brown eye. It is a good garden plant of medium height, with broad-based tapering spikes that have won many prizes for exhibitors (see **Figure 3.3**). **'Silver Jubilee'** is of similar vintage and has white florets with an intense black eye. The blooms are held high on rather tall stems, making it a plant for the back of a border. Our personal reservation about this cultivar is that it cannot be used in breeding for white flowers because it is a sport of 'Jumbo', a cultivar with blue-lavender flowers, and behaves like 'Jumbo' in respect of its colour when used as a parent in crosses.

'Olive Poppleton' and 'Rona' have often been used in delphinium breeding and both appear in the ancestry of the fine white delphinium **'Sandpiper'** (**AGM**). This has near-perfect white florets with a dark brown eye, regularly positioned on the stem to produce smooth-surfaced blooms. For many years it set the standards of bloom quality that we tried to match in our own seedlings. In the past we obtained superb results from plants raised from cuttings, but their vigour declined fairly quickly in subsequent years. 'Sandpiper' also seems to be subject to frost damage of early growth in spring. A white cultivar of our own raising, **'Lilian Bassett'** (**AGM**), has 'Olive Poppleton' as a grandparent but it was an unexpected result of crossing violet-flowered **'Emily Hawkins'** with an un-named blue. 'Lilian Bassett' has clear white flowers and an intense black eye in neat but short tapering spikes, with a plentiful supply of laterals (see **Figure 3.4**).

LEFT: **Figure 3.5. 'Elizabeth Cook' (AGM)**, with elegant long spikes of good white flowers, merits a place in any border.

ABOVE: **Figure 3.1c.**
Double flowers with more
than 13 sepals.

The flower stems have a tendency to be too thin and pliable to support the flowers, so need careful staking. The plant normally grows about 1 metre (39 inches) high, but among taller plants the leafy stems stretch upwards. **'Atholl' (AGM)** is another excellent garden delphinium that has white flowers with a black eye. The long blooms are columnar in form and generally have a short leafy stem, so the mature plant is of medium height.

There is a larger selection of white flowers with white eyes to choose from. **'Jill Curley'**, which has 'Rona' as one parent, is of medium height and has large flowers of good texture. The broad, tapered blooms are lovely when young, but their smooth and sleek surface is lost at maturity due to rumpling of the flowers as they age. **'Elisabeth Sahin'**, which is a selection from 'Jill Curley' x 'Rona', is a tall delphinium with long, slightly tapering blooms. The white flowers are of excellent form, and pale yellow hairs on the petals give the eye a yellowish tinge. **'Constance Rivett' (AGM)** is a plant of short to medium height with neat, tapering blooms of modest length above a compact mound of foliage, and is ideal for small gardens or positions at the front of a border. The white flowers are of good texture and have a ruffled edge.

Delphiniums related to 'Rona', such as **'Spindrift'**, are potential sources of cultivars with white flowers, and our cultivar **'Summerfield Ariane'**, named after the European series of space rockets, is an example. This medium-height plant, like 'Spindrift', is very early flowering, typically blooming two to three weeks before most named cultivars. It shares some of the less desirable features of 'Spindrift', such as the open-centred eye and the tendency for sepals to quill as the flowers age, which splits the previously complete disc of colour in a floret. Despite such imperfections, 'Ariane' is a vigorous plant that produces a nice group of flowers in borders. **'Elizabeth Cook' (AGM)** is another pure white delphinium with flowers that look rather like those of 'Ariane', although the blooms are usually longer and the plant is taller (see **Figure 3.5**). **'White Ruffles'** is a pure white of medium height, but with lovely flowers of fully double form (see Figure **3.1c**).

Named Delphiniums with Cream Flowers

Delphiniums with primrose-yellow flowers and yellow eyes are very attractive, and most delphinium breeders are tempted at some time to try to improve on existing cultivars. An ideal scheme would allow the colouring of *D. semibarbatum* to be incorporated without difficulty or detrimental effects. That is just a dream, and all that can be done is to work with Elatum cultivars that show the effect of a genetically recessive characteristic that turns off the normal pigmentation system of the flowers. This recessive gene frequently leads to extremely feeble plants with poor foliage and no merit, although their flowers and leaves usually have some yellowish pigmentation.

Finding delphiniums with creamy-white flowers that are also plants of acceptable standard is very difficult, and most selected cultivars have arisen by chance rather than from controlled breeding. The first named cultivar with cream flowers that we grew was **'Cream Cracker'**, which was discovered by an amateur grower as a self-sown seedling. The quite small flowers are flat and almost white with a faint yellowish tinge, but they have a neat primrose eye. We have kept the plant for more than 30 years, so it is a survivor, although not a vigorous grower.

After 'Cream Cracker' came **'Butterball'**, also with rather small florets but with neat, tapered blooms. In the RHS Delphinium Trial 'Butterball' always seems to be two-thirds foliage to one-third bloom, and in recent years flower quality seems to be in decline. It has been outshone by **'Sungleam' (AGM)**, which has larger florets of good quality and consistently good primrose colour (see **Figure 3.6**). The most recent cream from Blackmore & Langdon is **'Celebration' (AGM)**, which lacks the advantage of a yellow eye but has florets of lovely form and texture like parchment, linked with beautifully regular blooms on plants with good foliage (see **Figure 3.7**).

Surpassing all the previous cultivars, however, are **'Sunkissed' (AGM)**, which is derived from 'Sungleam' and has good long spikes of well-formed florets, and most recently **'Kennington Classic'**. Both cultivars can produce blooms of exhibition quality with good colour, and on plants with good foliage. These show that amateur breeders have a good chance of striking gold.

The search for yellow delphiniums has not been confined to Britain and, in the United States, Frank Reinelt made many attempts to produce a Pacific Hybrid Series with creamy yellow flowers, though without success. Other growers also select cultivars with cream flowers raised from imported seed, such as the 'New Millennium Hybrids' available from Dowdeswell in New Zealand. Two cultivars with yellow flowers, **'Meadowlark'** and **'Siskin'**, were obtained in this way and registered by Judith Miller of Washington State.

BELOW LEFT: **Figure 3.6.** In **'Sungleam' (AGM)** attractive primrose florets are enhanced by yellow eyes.

BELOW: **Figure 3.7.** **'Celebration' (AGM)** has a brown eye dominating creamy florets that have a parchment-like texture.

ABOVE LEFT: **Figure 3.8.**
One of the most beautiful
English delphiniums,
'Gillian Dallas' (AGM) has
pale-violet florets and a
white eye.

ABOVE RIGHT: **Figure 3.9.**
'Emily Hawkins' (AGM)
regularly produces well-
packed tapering spikes of
pale-violet florets with a
light-brown eye.

Named Delphiniums with Violet Flowers

Delphinium flowers that we consider as being violet include a wide range of shades, from pale colours – sometimes described as slate blue or pale grey – to light campanula violets and deeper colours. Starting with the palest, **'Walton Gemstone' (AGM)** has large, almost white flowers that are lightly tinted with a pinkish violet, and grows to about 1.7 metres (67 inches) tall. The eye is creamy white and there is deep violet staining of the back of the flowers and stems that shows up while the flowers are opening. **'Gillian Dallas' (AGM)** also has pale violet flowers but in a significantly deeper shade. The florets are of particularly good form, with a ruffled edge and neat white eye. They are also exceptionally large, being up to 90 millimetres (3½ inches) in diameter, and are evenly spaced in tapering blooms of fine form (see **Figure 3.8**). This is one of the most beautiful English delphiniums, growing to 1.5 metres (59 inches) or more in height, but it is advisable not to apply too much nitrogenous fertilizer, as the stems have a reputation for being susceptible to breakage. The white eye of both cultivars described so far is not a dramatic feature of the flowers, but it becomes very prominent when the violet is of a deeper shade, as in **'Walton Beauty'**. This has tapered spikes of well-formed violet florets with a white eye on compact plants, and should make a good garden plant when more widely distributed.

The colour of the eye can add greatly to the appeal of delphinium flowers, and this is true for **'Emily Hawkins' (AGM)**, which has a light-brown eye inherited from 'Olive Poppleton'. The nearly flat flowers are a pure, pale violet colour early in the year, but become bluer later in the season. The packing of flowers in the tapering blooms is usually immaculate and has made 'Emily Hawkins' a favourite with exhibitors (see **Figure 3.9**). It is a good garden plant growing to 1.8 metres (71 inches) tall, although the stem below the bloom tends to be rather too tall.

Excellent, broad spikes of pale violet flowers are a feature of **'Tiger Eye'**, which was named for the prominent patches of gold hairs on the black petals forming the eye (see **Figure 3.10**). The vigorous plants produce a plentiful supply of tapering blooms that grow to a height of 1.8 metres (71 inches). In the RHS Delphinium Trial at Wisley Gardens, these plants have been affected by mildew, and this is also a bad problem with **'Gordon Forsyth'**, an older cultivar that produces very long slender blooms of deeper violet flowers with a small dark-grey eye. 'Gordon Forsyth' is tall (2 metres/78 inches) and flowers rather late in the season. To control the mildew we have found it essential to spray the plants with systemic fungicide before the buds open. Similar problems afflict the much older cultivar **'Mighty Atom'**, and caused us to cease growing it. This is another delphinium with fairly long but slender blooms of large violet flowers that have a dark eye. The advantage over 'Gordon Forsyth' is that the flower stems below the bloom can be short, but we never found this in our garden, where the plant was grown among other herbaceous subjects.

For some obscure reason, strongly patterned colouring seems to occur quite frequently in delphiniums with violet flowers. **'Min' (AGM)** is one example, as the depth of the violet colour varies strongly between the edges and centre of the sepals. The flowers have a brown eye with some violet stripes, and are evenly spaced in long, broad blooms. In our garden, the plants seemed to need fairly frequent propagation.

Another variation in the appearance of flowers is for them to be double, and this is the case for **'Tiddles' (AGM)**. This has long, rather loosely packed blooms of partially double, light-violet flowers that sometimes have obvious petals distinguishable by flecks of dark grey. The plants grow to about 1.5 metres (59 inches) tall.

ABOVE: **Figure 3.10.** A black eye with prominent gold hairs dominates the pale-violet florets of **'Tiger Eye'**.

Named Delphiniums with Pastel Blue-Lavender Flowers

The flower colour most frequently seen in batches of seedlings grown from open-pollinated delphinium seed is probably pale blue overlaid with pinkish-lavender, so it is easy dismiss such flowers as 'nothing special'. One cultivar that just cannot be ignored in this way is **'Oliver' (AGM)**, because the nicely patterned colouring is so clear that the large florets, with their contrasting black eye, look fresh and transparent (see **Figure 3.11**). This impression is enhanced by the light and airy character of the blooms, on plants of medium height that flower early in the season. The flowers of **'Conspicuous' (AGM)** have generally similar colouring, with the superb dark brown eye attracting attention. The flowers are of good form and texture but pack closely together in fairly narrow long blooms of rather solid appearance. Having white eyes, rather than the sharply contrasting dark eyes of these two cultivars, results in visually rather uninteresting flowers, especially if these are packed closely together in large heavy blooms. **'Fanfare'** comes into this category, but is redeemed by having fairly blue flowers. It is best located at the back of a border, because it is a tall plant, often measuring 1.8 metres (71 inches).

'Spindrift' (AGM) is an early flowering cultivar that also has flowers of light blue overlaid with pinkish lavender, with an open-centred white eye, but the flowers are attractively ruffled at the edge. When first introduced in the early 1970s it was notable for a greeny-blue tinge to the colouring, but that now seems far less apparent. Nevertheless, 'Spindrift' is a fine garden plant up to 1.7 metres (67 inches) tall, with a good balance between the mound of foliage and the well-formed blooms.

RIGHT: **Figure 3.11.** A delightful delphinium, **'Oliver' (AGM)** has a fresh look in pale blue and lavender, with an intense black eye.

Named Delphiniums with Dusky-Pink Flowers

The arrival of the Pacific Hybrid **'Astolat'** series introduced delphinium flowers in shades of lilac-pink, a colour we prefer to call 'dusky pink'. Flowers in these shades soon appeared in English delphiniums. We grew and enjoyed the nicely formed, pale-pink flowers of **'Turkish Delight'**, and soon began using it as a parent for crosses. **'Strawberry Fair'** was the next introduction from Blackmore & Langdon, and was one of the first delphiniums ever to be granted Plant Breeder's Rights, which quite justifiably gave the raisers the right to obtain royalties on any propagation of this novelty. It is a deep, dusky pink with a white eye, and of medium height. Both cultivars remain available, and there are now also several later introductions to choose from. **'Langdon's Titania'** is a clear pink with a white eye (**Figure 3.12a**), while **'Cherub'** (AGM) is fairly tall and elegant with pale-pink flowers and a cream eye (**Figure 3.12b**). **'Pink Ruffles'** is unusual in having double flowers in pale pink on a compact plant of medium height. **'Foxhill Nina'** produces many neat spikes of light-pink, rounded flowers. **'Langdon's Royal Flush'** (AGM) has darker dusky-pink flowers with a white eye, and can produce fairly large blooms, while **'Cymbeline'** has large, deep-pink flowers that tend to stay cupped. It has a white eye on plants 1.7 metres (67 inches) tall.

Our own breeding of dusky pinks began with 'Turkish Delight', and seed of the cross ('Turkish Delight' x 'Strawberry Fair'). Our most successful selection and introduction has been **'Rosemary Brock'** (AGM), named after our neighbour, who allowed us to grow seedlings in her garden. This is a plant of medium height, with well-formed dusky-pink florets that have a brown eye; the blooms are smooth and tapered (see **Figure 3.12c**). It is an excellent garden plant that has also won many prizes when blooms are used for exhibition. 'Rosemary Brock' has often been used in breeding for dusky pinks, and is one parent of **'Lucia Sahin'** (AGM), which set new standards for the intensity of the mulberry-pink colour obtainable in delphinium flowers (see **Figure 3.12d**). The deep colour is allied to blooms of excellent form that can be very large when grown for exhibition, although the plant is good in the garden but quite tall (2.2 metres/87 inches). **'Clifford Lass'** is another cultivar very similar in colour and style to 'Rosemary Brock'. It should be noted that the colour of these cultivars is prone to fading in strong sunshine.

While efforts to breed even darker dusky pinks continue, pale pinks are also of interest and look good with a contrasting dark eye. **'Darling Sue'** is fascinating in having reddish colouring of the stems, and a home decorator's 'hint of pink' tint on the large, almost white flowers with a prominent black eye. It is very early flowering and makes a good plant to grow in a pot for a conservatory (see **Figure 5.6** on page 92). For almost perfectly round florets in pale pink with a neat dark eye **'Summerfield Miranda'** (AGM) is hard to beat, but it grows to about 1.8 metres (71 inches) tall (see **Figure 3.12e**). **'Our Deb'** (AGM) is a flower of very different style, with medium-size, light-pink florets that have an attractive frilly edge (see **Figure 3.12f**). The flowers have very long stalks and are widely spaced in broad tapering blooms.

One of the latest delphiniums to flower, **'Summerfield Diana'** has well-formed florets with a dark eye and marked shading of the pale pink colour of the sepals (see **Figure 3.13**). A recent introduction, **'Shottesbrooke Lady'**, is also late flowering and produces fine blooms of pale-pink flowers with a dark eye.

OPPOSITE: **Figure 3.12.** Images of florets that illustrate the range of colour and form available in delphinium cultivars with dusky-pink flowers.

RIGHT: **Figure 3.12a.**
'Langdon's Titania'.

FAR RIGHT: **Figure 3.12b.**
'Cherub' (AGM).

RIGHT: **Figure 3.12c.**
'Rosemary Brock' (AGM).

FAR RIGHT: **Figure 3.12d.**
'Lucia Sahin' (AGM).

RIGHT: **Figure 3.12e.**
'Summerfield Miranda'
(AGM).

FAR RIGHT: **Figure 3.12f.**
'Our Deb' (AGM).

LEFT: **Figure 3.13.** Late-flowering **'Summerfield Diana'** has well-formed pale-pink florets with a striking dark eye.

Named Delphiniums with Purple Flowers

We have noted already that introductions of named delphiniums during the past thirty years have come primarily from amateur raisers and, for purples, this is especially significant because cultivars introduced 40 to 50 years ago have effectively vanished from the scene. We recall, for example, spectacular blooms of **'Sabu'** on the show bench at the first shows we visited, but like many purple-flowered cultivars it proved to be short-lived and was soon unobtainable.

The nearest equivalent to 'Sabu' available today is **'Bruce' (AGM)**, which responds well to heavy feeding and can produce enormous blooms suitable for exhibition. The blooms look especially nice before full development, when the deep violet-purple colour of the florets, with their dark brown eyes, is still fresh and gleaming, and the broad spike tapers to a point (see **Figure 3.14a**). 'Bruce' also makes a vigorous garden plant, growing to about 1.8 metres (71 inches) and producing a good display of high-quality flowers. Fortunately, this fine cultivar is not abnormally susceptible to mildew. **'Michael Ayres' (AGM)** is another purple with dark eye, although the flowers have deep-blue outer sepals and the purple of the inner sepals lacks lustre (see **Figure 3.14b**). Up to about 1.8 metres (71 inches) tall with nicely tapered blooms, this cultivar flowers earlier than 'Bruce'. The best choice for a really brilliant purple with black eye is **'Purple Velvet'**. The large, flat florets are held in quite narrow long blooms with hard stems. A recent introduction, **'Amadeus'**, provides flowers with a large brown eye set on purple inner sepals over a dark-blue background. The plants are of medium height, about 1.5 metres (59 inches) tall.

Dark purple flowers probably look most dramatic when there is a white eye to light up the colour. An example of this is **'Chelsea Star'**, with very large deep-violet-purple florets that have a stunning white eye in broad tapering spikes that can soar upwards from a short leafy stem (see **Figure 3.14c**). It can be so spectacular that some delphinium enthusiasts forgive its extreme susceptibility to mildew. If it succumbs you must spray it with systemic fungicide, or the whole plant, including the flowers, is ruined in most years by the white coating produced by the fungus.

In the early 1970s, the purples of Pacific Hybrids were beautiful, and crossing a selected plant of the **'King Arthur'** series

Figure 3.14. Images of florets that illustrate some purple delphinium cultivars:

BELOW LEFT:
Figure 3.14a. 'Bruce' (AGM).

BELOW RIGHT:
Figure 3.14b. 'Michael Ayres' (AGM).

with the very deep-violet-purple 'Sentinel' gave a good purple-flowered seedling with a white eye. That selected seedling was one parent of **'Summerfield Oberon'**, which produces broad tapering spikes of purple flowers with white eyes. This cultivar flowers early in the season, when the brilliance and depth of the purple is superb (see **Figure 3.14d**). Unfortunately, it can grow rather tall (2.2 metres/87 inches), and the slender stems are then susceptible to wind damage.

Named Delphiniums with Multicoloured Flowers

There are always flowers in colours that defy easy classification into groups, however loosely defined, and we shall escape this quandary by calling them multicoloured.

Our first example is **'Giotto' (AGM, Figure 3.14e)**, which is like one of its parents, **'Cassius' (AGM, Figure 3.14f)**, in being difficult to classify as a purple flower. In most seasons the flowers develop brilliant blue stripes along the centres of each sepal that brighten up the otherwise rather dull purple. A light brown eye also helps to make the flowers attractive and with long blooms of good form on

compact plants it is a useful delphinium for the garden.

Another curiously coloured cultivar is **'Franjo Sahin'**, which again shows the characteristics of one parent, **'Min'**, in the patterning of the flower colour. The patterning is very strong, but the colour is neither violet nor purple. The blooms are of good form, although when we see this cultivar at Wisley there is some suspicion that the bottom florets drop more quickly than those of 'Min' do. It has to be a matter of personal choice whether you would want the flowers in your garden, as this plant would be hard to blend in harmoniously with others. However, it might well be attractive to adventurous florists.

'Can Can' (AGM) is also unusual, with double flowers of similar size to the flowers of most current named cultivars. It is named for its rather frilly set of inner sepals and petals that are a deep mauve in colour, cupped within the skirt of the dark-blue outer sepals. The blooms are large and the plant grows up to 1.9 metres (75 inches) tall although, like 'Franjo Sahin', it might be difficult to place relative to other flowers in a border.

Floristry is the major application for the remaining multicoloured cultivars, which

ABOVE LEFT: **Figure 3.14c.** **'Chelsea Star'**.

ABOVE RIGHT: **Figure 3.14d.** **'Summerfield Oberon'**.

all have double flowers. The first is the venerable **'Alice Artindale'**, which has pretty little rosebud double flowers in pink and blue shades held tight against the stems. If this is ever successfully tissue-cultured, it might be hugely popular with growers of flowers for cutting. However, 'Alice' is not the only rosebud double, as **'Susan Edmunds'** has larger flowers that are of similar form. The colour is best described as pale violet and the flowers have only short stalks, so that the blooms are rather narrow. This delphinium first appeared as a self-sown seedling in the garden of Mr E Edmunds at Chalfont St Giles, Buckinghamshire, UK, so it is always worthwhile to be on the lookout for interesting novelties.

Delphiniums with double flowers are among the seed selections developed in New Zealand by Dowdeswell, and the cultivar **'Sarita'** is of this type, its pink-tinged inner sepals and petals over pale-blue outer sepals giving very attractive flowers. The flowers are quite large, and are held on stalks of sufficient length for the bloom to be of normal form. **'Dunsden Green'** is another cultivar with flowers that do not have the usual distinction between sepals and petals. The flower has many 'petals' and is double, although it has an open centre with the carpels exposed. The colour is a creamy white with a very pronounced green tinge that makes the flowers interesting, if rather untidy. The plants appear vigorous and provide a good display of flowers.

Named Delphiniums with Blue Flowers

Looking back to the days when we first became delphinium enthusiasts brings to mind a Blackmore & Langdon cultivar, **'Maritime'**, which had large florets of intense, deep gentian blue with a black eye. We grew this for several years from a plant in a huge pot carried home from a stand at the Chelsea Flower Show. The individual florets were lovely, but the narrow blooms were often irregular and the plant was not very vigorous. We have made many crosses trying to obtain better plants, but these features seem to plague deep gentian blues. One comparable cultivar is **'Thamesmead' (AGM)**. Taller plants with long blooms are **'Fenella' (AGM)**, introduced in 1960, and the almost identical **'Nicholas Woodfield'**, which both provide gentian blue flowers with a black eye. 'Fenella' has been a very long-lived plant in our garden, although the florets are rather small for our taste (see

Figure 3.15.
Images of florets of some blue delphiniums.

LEFT: **Figure 3.15a.**
'Fenella' (AGM).

LEFT: **Figure 3.15b.**
'Clifford Sky' (AGM).

Figure 3.15a). A more recent introduction is **'David Mannion' (AGM)**, which also has Fenella-style florets in tapering spikes, but on a shorter plant.

It is possible to obtain even darker blues than 'Fenella', although this is usually at the expense of colour purity. A good example is the very popular **'Faust' (AGM)**, which can produce long slender blooms on plants up to 2.5 metres (99 inches) tall that look wonderful in the grand herbaceous borders of stately homes. Under some conditions it can appear brilliantly blue, and used as a parent it can yield plants with beautiful clear-blue flowers but, in reality, the rather untidy flower is heavily tinged with purple. It is reputed to be a very durable perennial but in our garden the plant succumbed to crown rot after three years. If you are happy with the colour of 'Faust' but not with the height, then the dwarf cultivar **'Blue Tit'** is possibly ideal for you. This was the first short-growing delphinium introduced by Blackmore & Langdon but, as for 'Faust', the florets are often rather rough. It is possible that floret quality has declined over the many years that 'Blue Tit' has been in cultivation, but with slender, tough stems it is well suited to small gardens or rather windy sites.

Returning to clear deep-blue delphinium flowers, but now ones with the sepal colour lit up by white petals, **'Blue Nile' (AGM)** continues to set the standard against which other cultivars are judged. It is not the most reliable performer in terms of spike perfection, and the florets are only of medium size, but the colour clarity is outstanding.

For clear, pale blues, the large florets of **'Pericles'** and **'Clifford Sky' (AGM)** are particularly beautiful (see **Figure 3.15b**), as they have the same smooth form as those of 'Blue Nile'. These cultivars flower some two to three weeks later than most named delphiniums. Both can also produce blooms up to 1.3 metres (51 inches) long on plants of modest height. **'Skyline'** is another late-flowering cultivar with attractive pale-blue flowers that are almost fully double in form.

There are, of course, many named delphiniums with flowers that can be described as mid-blue. We first became actively involved in delphinium breeding in the late 1960s when the RHS Delphinium Trial at Wisley Gardens regularly contained entries from amateur raiser Tom Cowan, including several with blue flowers named for the lochs of his native land. Plants of **'Loch Nevis'** were a wonderful sight, with many long blooms of ruffled sky-blue flowers and white eyes. On the show bench too, blooms of 'Loch Nevis' overpowered all competition. This old-timer is still available and is a good plant for the back of a border, while **'Loch Leven' (AGM)**, another sky blue with a white eye, is much shorter, and thus better for small gardens (see **Figure 3.15c**). These two blues have been widely used by delphinium breeders.

BELOW: **Figure 3.15c.** '**Loch Leven' (AGM).**

FAR LEFT: **Figure 3.15d.** **'Langdon's Blue Lagoon' (AGM).**

LEFT: **Figure 3.15e.** **'Leonora'.**

RIGHT: **Figure 3.17.** **'Langdon's Pandora' (AGM)** is a recent introduction with rather small pale-blue florets and a blue eye striped with black.

LEFT: **Figure 3.16.** **'Lord Butler' (AGM)** is a popular garden delphinium of medium height with flat-surfaced blooms of mid-blue.

'Langdon's Blue Lagoon' (AGM) is another lovely blue with a white eye that traces its ancestry to these cultivars. This is a plant of medium height with frilled flowers that tend to tilt slightly upwards (see **Figure 3.15d**).

Two other blues with white eyes deserve a mention. The first is **'Lord Butler' (AGM)**, a plant of medium height with relatively small flowers that have sepals curving backwards. The florets are always perfectly positioned so that the tapered blooms are flat-surfaced (see **Figure 3.16**). The second is **'Leonora'**, with beautiful large flowers that are well displayed on slender stems (see **Figure 3.15e**). The problem is inconsistency: while some growers find this cultivar reliable and long-lived, others find that it lacks vigour.

Staying with light blues, but flowers with dark eyes, **'Blue Dawn' (AGM)** is a vigorous old favourite in the traditional style for the back of herbaceous borders. It is rather tall (2 metres/78 inches) and produces many long, narrow spires of pink-flushed sky-blue flowers with a black eye. **'Langdon's Pandora' (AGM)** is a more recent introduction of similar style, although the rather small florets are a clear pale blue (see **Figure 3.17**). **'Walton Benjamin'** also has quite small flowers but in a much brighter blue and with a broader spike than 'Pandora', although the eyes of both are blue, striped with black. The

LEFT: **Figure 3.15f.**
'Galileo' (AGM).

naming of selected delphinium cultivars is not purely a British activity, and we note here **'Kotariasia Elotaivaalla'**, a cultivar similar to 'Pandora' with sky-blue flowers and a greyish-brown eye having occasional blue stripes on the petals. This was registered in 2002 by Vesa Koivu, a grower in Finland, where delphiniums grow well. The name, which means 'Starlings on an August Sky', describes the impression given by the flowers.

For a final group of blue cultivars we include three that first attracted the attention of delphinium enthusiasts when winning prizes as exhibition blooms. Our own introduction, **'Galileo' (AGM)**, produces long tapering blooms of mid-blue flowers with a black eye (see **Figure 3.15f**). It has been very successful in the RHS Trial of Delphiniums at Wisley Gardens, twice winning the Stuart Ogg medal for the best display. Even so, the colour does not match our ideal – set by 'Maritime' – because when the flowers open they are heavily flushed with deep mauve. In most seasons this mauve flush usually disappears as the

flowers develop. Another delphinium with a similar problem is the wonderfully reliable garden plant **'Cassius' (AGM)**, which never seems certain if it should have gentian blue or purple flowers (see **Figure 3.14f**). The broad-based tapering blooms are of excellent form and rise from a very compact mound of foliage to give a plant of medium height. In our garden it has generally developed to a good blue rather than remaining purple, but this probably varies with soil and the season.

'Carol Fishenden' is a pale blue with dark eyes and attracts attention because the relatively small flowers pack neatly together to produce a beautifully smooth-surfaced bloom in the style of 'Lord Butler'. Young flowers show some pink flush at the base of the sepals and it will be interesting to see how this cultivar fares in the RHS Trial for the Award of Garden Merit (AGM). **'After Midnight'** accompanies 'Carol Fishenden' in the Trial to assess if it is a star performer as a garden plant. This striking delphinium has large florets of good form in a mixture of dark blue and purple, and with a black eye rather like 'Faust', though the bloom is much broader. **'Gertrude Sahin'** is another blue on trial for garden merit after success on the show-bench. This has large florets with translucent, pale-blue pointed sepals and a white eye. We include these three cultivars because they may be stars for the future as potential replacements for elderly stalwarts of the border now in their declining years.

Elatum-group Seed Selections in Commerce

Hand pollination provides a delphinium breeder with the only approach that determines the parentage of a seed with absolute certainty. A seed producer can influence the nature of plants obtainable from seed by choosing parents having the desired characteristics, as described in chapter 4. More generally, pollination occurs naturally through the activities of insect pollinators such as bees or hummingbirds, which are attracted to the flowers by nectar in the petal spurs and in the process receive a dusting of pollen, which they are then likely to shake off at the succeeding flowers they visit. Such pollination is termed open pollination. In this case, a flower may be self-pollinated by pollen displaced from anthers within the same floret or by pollen brought by insects from other flowers of the plant. If insects pollinate the flowers, they would also be likely to bring pollen from other delphiniums in the vicinity, which may be of a different variety or species, causing out-crossing. When delphiniums flower in an open field or garden, the open-pollinated seed collected from them is thus of uncertain parentage.

The extent of out-crossing in open pollination is an important issue when delphiniums of inferior quality grow near to named delphiniums. If out-crossing to the poor-quality delphiniums occurs, seed from the selected plants would yield some inferior plants. Unwanted features, such as wild-type single flowers or irregular floret placement, are frequently genetically dominant relative to desirable qualities of the seed parent, and would thus show up in

the seedlings. This fact emphasizes the need for inferior delphiniums to be removed from the vicinity where delphiniums are grown for seed production. The high proportion of inferior plants produced by much delphinium seed sold to gardeners unfortunately suggests that poor plants were present in the fields used for seed production.

Colour Mixtures

Open-pollinated seed harvested from delphinium specialists' collections of named cultivars, or breeders' stocks of selected cultivars, provide a source of delphiniums of good quality. Particular examples are the seeds available from Blackmore & Langdon in the UK and the 'New Century Hybrids' line from Sahin in Holland. These hybrids have named delphiniums of British origin as their principal forebears, and provide what are sometimes called 'English delphiniums'.

Single Colour-Seed Selections

Seed selections providing high-quality delphiniums that came true to colour from seed appeared first in the United States, when the Californian firm of Vetterle & Reinelt introduced their 'Pacific Hybrid' delphinium series. The quality and colour range of these selections steadily improved from their introduction in 1935 until 1970, and they influenced delphinium breeding and seed supplies all over the world.

Pacific Hybrids

The story of the development of 'Pacific Hybrids' is an interesting one that emphasizes how closely these American delphiniums are related to English delphiniums. As a new emigrant from Czechoslovakia in 1926, Frank Reinelt was greatly impressed by the enormous blooms of a group of seedlings from a famous Blackmore & Langdon cultivar, **'Millicent Blackmore'**, that he saw in California. He resolved to try his hand at breeding delphiniums and began immediately in the way that any gardener can. He purchased packets of seed from Vanderbilt, an American specialist noted for the thin, hard stems of his plants, and from British specialists Blackmore & Langdon and Watkin Samuel, whose plants had exceptionally long flower spikes. He was soon making crosses between selected plants, obtaining flowers in lavender and violet shades with a few blues. Pure whites were introduced by using seed from the American raiser Charles Barber's 'Hoodacre Whites', which was also derived from plants of English origin. Within four years, Reinelt's delphiniums were being sold commercially as the 'Pacific Strain'.

Frank Reinelt became a partner in Vetterle & Reinelt, of Capitola, California, in 1934. The Company was mainly concerned with breeding tuberous begonias, but Reinelt continued breeding delphiniums, growing 5,000 seedlings a year. The original aim was to select individual seedlings and propagate them from cuttings, as had been done in England. Economic considerations, and serious plant losses caused by a late-summer infection with 'aster yellows' carried by leafhoppers, forced a change of approach. The breeding programme, discussed in more detail in chapter 4, was then directed towards raising a series of colour lines that would come true to colour from seed, because Reinelt felt that growing delphiniums as annuals was more appropriate for the climate of many regions of the United States.

Reinelt was also innovative in attempting to introduce new colours, for example by using X-ray treatment of the seed of the red-flowered species *D. cardinale* in order to obtain seedlings that could be crossed with plants of the 'Pacific Hybrid' lines. Although failing to produce red-flowered delphiniums, Reinelt considered that the use of the *D. cardinale* seedlings resulted in more vivid blues and purples, and brought a rich, velvety brilliance to **'Black Knight'**. The 'Astolat' series, with dusky-pink flowers, was another result of this work.

Frank Reinelt was an outstandingly successful delphinium breeder, and we give below his own descriptions of the flowers of each of the Pacific Hybrid series, which were mostly given names chosen from Tennyson's *Idylls of the King*. The names remain in common use all over the world,

but sadly the quality of the delphiniums to which the labels are attached seldom match the quality of the originals.

'Lancelot' series: 'A clear lilac self [a uniformly coloured flower] with white bee [eye]. Well-balanced spikes with large flowers of fine round form.'

'Guinevere' series: 'A clear, pink-lavender self with white bee. Very large individual flowers averaging up to three inches [7.5 centimetres] in diameter.'

'Camelliard' series: 'Bi-colour lavender with white bee, possessing classical perfection of form of the individual flowers, which are very round and attain very large size, averaging three inches [7.5 centimetres] in diameter.'

'King Arthur' series: 'Beautifully formed, long spikes of rich, royal purple flowers with a velvety texture and large white bee carried on thin, woody stems.'

'Black Knight' series: 'The darkest violet, with black bee. Individual flowers two and one-half to three inches [6.5–7.5 centimetres] in diameter, of beautiful round form, with heavy velvety texture, which gives the colour luminosity and vividness not seen before in Delphiniums. Very long, well-formed spikes.'

'Astolat' series: 'Colour variations extend from pale blush through all shades of lilac pink to deep raspberry rose with large fawn and black eyes for contrast.'

'Galahad' series: 'Clear white flowers, often three inches [7.5 centimetres] in diameter, with white bees combined with glistening, heavy texture.'

'Percival' series: 'Large, glistening white flowers with strongly contrasting black bees, beautifully spaced on long, tapering spikes.'

'Summer Skies' series: 'Light heavenly blue of a summer sky, with white bees representing the fleecy clouds.'

'Blue Bird' series: 'Well-formed round flowers, two and one-half inches [6.5 centimetres] in diameter in clear medium blues, with white bees on very long, graceful spikes.'

'Blue Jay' series: 'Clear medium to dark blue; very intense and alive, with dark, contrasting bee.'

'**Round Table' series:** 'This selection was not simply a mixture of seeds of the other Series but included seeds from several hundred different crosses made in the course of the breeding programme for new colours and improvement of the colour lines.'

Even before 1970, in the period when Pacific Hybrid delphiniums were at their finest, it was commonplace for delphinium specialists in Britain to claim that the plants were not very good perennials. In a sense that is an irrelevant criticism, provided one accepts that these delphiniums were meant to be grown as annuals, providing superb blooms within a few months of sowing. Unfortunately it remains true that Pacific Hybrids, and seed selections derived from them, cannot be considered reliable perennials. A more serious problem is that 35 years after development of the Pacific Hybrid colour lines ceased, plants raised from seeds that are sold under the same name are often of very poor quality, bearing little resemblance to the originals.

Seed Selections from Europe

In recent years, a few delphinium specialists in Europe have developed seed selections that aim to provide Elatum delphiniums true to colour, with the bloom characteristics and perenniality typical of English-named cultivars. The quickest route is to supply seed from hand-pollinated crosses between specific cultivars, rather than to develop a true-breeding colour line, as done by Reinelt.

The '**Southern' series**, registered in 1991, included ten distinct colour groups and was a notable but short-lived effort resulting from collaboration between amateur enthusiasts L T Harrison and Duncan McGlashan. The seed was produced by hand-pollination, and three of the colour groups gained an AGM in the Royal Horticultural Society's Trial of Delphiniums from seed in 1994. '**Southern Maidens'** (with white flowers), '**Southern Countrymen'** (with blue flowers), and '**Southern Countess'** (with pink flowers) produced excellent groups of plants, with blooms of high quality. A feature of this trial was the high winter losses among groups of plants of 'Pacific Hybrid' origin.

The '**Centurion' series** F1 seed selections introduced by Dutch seed supplier Sahin, results from collaboration with British raiser Duncan McGlashan, who gained an AGM in the 1994 RHS Trial with '**Zeeland Light Blues'**. The first introductions, '**Centurion Sky Blue'** (1997) and '**Centurion White'** (1998), have been followed by '**Gentian Blue' F1** (2004) and '**Rose Shades' F1** (2005). These strains reliably produce delphiniums comparable in quality with the named English delphiniums used in their production. In our experience, seedlings from 'Centurion White' can produce blooms of exhibition quality.

Seed Selections from New Zealand

'**New Millennium' F1** hybrid seed selections for a range of colours have been introduced by Terry Dowdeswell in New Zealand. He has selected cultivars that grow well under the local climatic conditions, having started from seed of crosses between English named cultivars. Single colour selections include '**Royal Aspirations'**, for deep blues with white eyes, '**Blushing Brides'**, yielding a mixture of mulberry pinks, '**Pagan Purples'**, for dark blue/purple flowers with ruffled or nearly double form, and '**Innocence'**, for pure whites with white eye. Dowdeswell seems more adventurous than other growers in seeking out flowers with unusual form, and has introduced seed strains that yield eyeless double flowers.

Seed Selections for Dwarf Delphiniums

Seed selections mentioned so far mainly yield plants 1.4–2 metres (55–78 inches) tall, which are often criticized as too tall and requiring too much staking for the average garden. Considerable attention has therefore been given to the breeding of shorter delphiniums. The cultivar '**Blue Tit'** was the first short-growing cultivar introduced by Blackmore & Langdon, and was followed by several others in different colours, between them providing a group of possible parents for short-growing cultivars. Plants of unusually short stature also arose within collections of 'Pacific Hybrids', and these have been widely exploited in the development of short-growing selections, particularly in the United States.

'Blue Fountains' Group

The **'Blue Fountains'** delphiniums, introduced in 1978 by the British seed wholesaler Hurst, was one of the earliest seed-raised selections that yielded short-growing plants. Ralph Gould, the plant breeder for Hurst, began developing shorter delphiniums in the early 1950s by raising seedlings from selected 'Pacific Hybrids' with unusually short, whippy stems, which made them more resistant to wind damage than the normal tall plants. At a later stage, crosses were made with short-growing English cultivars such as 'Blue Tit' and selected seedlings from the Hurst 'Monarch' line, to add their hardiness and perennial character. The resulting 'Blue Fountains' delphiniums thus combined desirable features of both British and American delphinium cultivars.

During development of 'Blue Fountains', a particularly short, sturdy delphinium with very attractive semi-double, mid-blue flowers and a white bee was selected. It was found to reproduce remarkably true to type from seed and was introduced by Hurst as **'Blue Heaven'** in 1980.

Seed of both 'Blue Fountains' and 'Blue Heaven' is still available. However, the newer **'Magic Fountains'** series provides a large number of different colour selections that come true to colour. The plants come to flower very quickly from sowing, and readily repeat flower in their first season. Unfortunately, our personal experience with plants raised from seed or purchased from nurseries is that the flowers are of unreliable quality.

Delphiniums for Cut-flower Production

A growing demand for delphiniums as flowers for cutting has been a major factor driving the development of delphinium seed selections in recent years. In general, the demand is for plants that come quickly to flower from seed, with narrow cylindrical or slightly tapered blooms of moderate length. One example is the **'Clear Springs'** series, available in a number of distinct colour lines developed from plants of 'Pacific Hybrid' origin. While such strains may be used as glass-house crops, they can also be used as garden flowers.

Other examples are the F1 **'Guardian'** series and the F1 **'Aurora'** series, which provide *elatum*-hybrid-type delphiniums that come true to colour from seed but with the early cropping and repeat-flowering characteristics that are useful for cut-flower production. Experience with the **'Aurora'** F1 deep-purple series in our garden was of very early flowering plants with large flowers of brilliant, luminous colour, but imperfect floret form for both the purple and F1 lavender series. Under the conditions of a normal English winter the plants started into growth too early in the year, and all died after suffering frost damage, so they should not be regarded as reliably perennial.

Elatum-group Seed Selections: Conclusions

It is not difficult for a delphinium enthusiast to produce seed that will yield new plants with some desired characteristic – for example white flowers with a black eye – by making a cross between suitable parents. A high-quality commercial seed strain should provide plants that are also uniform with respect to plant architecture as well as less easily defined qualities of the flowers such as colour clarity, sepal form and texture, so that they have a distinctive character. One of the greatest triumphs of Frank Reinelt's breeding of 'Pacific Hybrids' was that he achieved exactly this distinctive identity for open-pollinated seed strains, with the names 'Black Knight' and 'King Arthur' becoming as tightly linked to flower character as 'Blue Nile'. It is an open question whether any currently available seed strains for tall or dwarf *elatum* hybrids will ever attain such distinction. Rapidly changing fashion and economics do not favour steady improvement of seed strains by ruthless reselection of seed parent stocks over many generations.

Belladonna Group

The original **'Belladonna'** delphinium was first cultivated around 1857 and was, incorrectly, accorded species status as *D. belladonna* when it was offered for sale in the catalogue of the British growers Kelways in 1881. These plants were about 90 centimetres (35 inches) in height with branching stems bearing single, pale-blue flowers that were sterile; stocks were maintained by regular propagation. Around 1902–03 a few seed pods were found on a 'Belladonna' plant, and two new cultivars selected from the seedlings raised, **'Grandiflora'** and **'Mrs G. Gibson'**, were fertile. In the hands of the Dutch nurseryman Bonne Ruys, further offspring, including the light blue **'Capri'** and its white mutation **'Moerheimi'** (see **Figure 3.18a**), were obtained, and still remain in cultivation a century later.

Figure 3.18.
Belladonna-type delphiniums.

RIGHT: **Figure 3.18a.**
'Moerheimi'.

The origin of **'Belladonna'** is unknown, and the sterility of the plant was a puzzle to the early growers. It was suggested that hybridization between plants with different numbers of chromosomes, for example a cross between a tetraploid *elatum* hybrid and a diploid species such as *D. grandiflorum*, could result in infertile triploid hybrids. Gustav Mehlquist, an American professor of horticultural science writing in 1963, concluded that this was probably the correct explanation after detailed studies of crosses between a white-flowered Elatum cultivar and either of the diploid species *D. grandiflorum* or *D. tatsienense*. The resulting hybrids all had blue flowers and were of similar character to commercially available belladonna types. Mehlquist's hybrids were infertile triploids but, after treatment with colchicine to cause chromosome doubling, the resulting hexaploid hybrids crossed freely with the available commercial belladonna types. Mehlquist also concluded that the development of new belladonna delphiniums was likely to be an unrewarding field for plant breeders because he had found it exceedingly difficult to raise any plants of belladonna type that were significantly better or different from those already available.

The ever-increasing popularity of delphiniums as cut flowers has led to renewed public interest in belladonna delphiniums, which have always been highly regarded as flowers for cutting. Stems of the gentian blue flowers of **'Volkerfrieden'** (**AGM**), a belladonna of German origin, must alone represent a large proportion of delphiniums sold by florists (see **Figure 3.18b**). This situation has naturally encouraged plant breeders to seek new cultivars of similar style. There is now a steady stream of new introductions from breeders in the United States, Japan and the Netherlands that will mostly be seen first in the florists' shops of the world rather than as flowers in our gardens. Despite being sterile, 'Volkerfrieden' itself is one source, because the gentian-blue colour is not very stable and mutations with flowers in violet or purplish shades occur.

'**Delft Blue**', for example, provides pretty violet-blue flowers with white edges, and fortunately this has been available for gardeners since its introduction in 2003.

We have found **'Atlantis'** (**AGM**) to be the most reliable of the belladonna delphiniums that we have grown. Plants quickly reached a large size, developing many stems and a mass of dark inky-blue flowers earlier than most of our Elatum cultivars. Our only reservation is that the flowers are at the top of rather tall leafy stems (see **Figure 3.18c**).

It is appropriate at this point to mention delphiniums raised from the **'Connecticut Yankees'** seed mixture, although their origin differs from that of older belladonna cultivars. The famous American photographer Edward Steichen, who was also a delphinium breeder, used several dwarf species as well as belladonna cultivars in his breeding experiments. The seed mixture yields plants with extensively branched, slender stems and with large

ABOVE: **Figure 3.18b.** **'Volkerfrelden'** (**AGM**).

RIGHT: **Figure 3.18c.**
'Atlantis' (AGM).

florets in a range of blues, lavenders and whites that made very pretty plants in our borders (see **Figure 3.18d**).

There are several other selections of Belladonna-group delphiniums that flower well in the first season from seed. Our favourite is **'Casa Blanca'**, which has white flowers that provide a lovely display on compact plants in the first year. Mature plants develop many rather tall stems and provide a long-lasting display, with flowers opening in sequence as the secondary branches develop. If the stems are cut down when the first flowers are over, the plants also repeat-flower in August or September (this and all other months mentioned in the book are as for the northern hemisphere; add six months to apply to the southern hemisphere).

A good proportion of seedlings from the seed selection **'Oriental Blue'** have flowers of a brilliant gentian blue, but we find the colour shows seasonal variation. It can be strongly tinged with purple, just as 'Volkerfrieden' and some other belladonna cultivars are.

LEFT: **Figure 3.18d.** A white seedling from **'Connecticut Yankees'**.

Grandiflorum Group

Cultivated in gardens for around two centuries, these dwarf delphiniums take their name from the large-flowered Siberian larkspur *D. grandiflorum*. Originally reported by Johannes Amman, *D. grandiflorum* was one of the six species of delphinium included by Linnaeus when he introduced the binomial method of plant classification in 1753. Described from the Transbaykal region in Siberia, this delphinium lives on stony slopes and the dry meadows of river valleys in Mongolia, Manchuria and north-western China. Further east in China, *D. grandiflorum* tends to be dwarfer in habit, and with larger flowers. The plants here were originally thought to be of a different species, named *D. chinense* by Friedrich Fischer in 1824, but they were later recognized as a variant of *D. grandiflorum*. When a species like *D. grandiflorum* spreads over such a vast area, small differences arise in the plants, and these differences may persist in localized regions well separated from the first population to be described. The rules of botanical nomenclature declare that the earliest given name should have precedence, so all forms of this species should be called *D. grandiflorum* L. However, the name of *D. chinense* remains in commercial seed catalogues to this day, which leads to confusion. The dwarfer form with larger flowers is considered more desirable by gardeners, and it can be thought of as *D. grandiflorum* v. *chinense*, even if this is not botanically correct.

D. grandiflorum was in cultivation in Europe as early as 1758. The seed catalogues of Vilmorin-Andrieux Co. show that both single-flowered and double-flowered forms were listed in 1824, while by 1880, Haage & Schmidt listed 11 forms of *D. chinense*, as well as *D. grandiflorum*. Seed catalogues of today do not show such variety, although the bright blue 'Blue Butterfly', which first appeared around 1907, is still available (**Figure 3.19a**), as are 'Blauer Zwerg' (Blue Dwarf) and the paler 'Sky Blue'. Present-day selections

Figure 3.19.
Some dwarf delphiniums.

RIGHT: **Figure 3.19a.**
D. grandiflorum '**Blue Butterfly**'.

LEFT: **Figure 3.19b.**
D. grandiflorum **'Amour'.**

include **'Summer Blues'** in pale blue, **'Summer Nights'** in a good gentian blue and **'Summer Stars'** with white flowers. Another interesting selection listed as *D. grandiflorum* is **'Amour'** (**Figure 3.19b**) or **'Butterfly Mixed'**, which will provide you with flowers in pink and white as well as blue. The gentian blue, **'Blue Pygmy'**, and the **'Tom Pouce'** series, ('Gentian Blue', 'Sky Blue' and 'Snow White') are listed as *D. chinense* (**Figure 3.19c**).

Perhaps the most spectacular cultivated form of *D. grandiflorum* is **'Blue Mirror'**, a pure light gentian-blue flower that lacks a spur and tends to face upwards. A selection made early in the last century, 'Blue Mirror' was variously called *D. cineraria*, *D. cineraria coeruleum* or *D. chinense cineraria coeruleum*! Careful isolation and selection of plants is required to maintain such a mutation, and it is not easy to find in seed catalogues.

All these varieties of *D. grandiflorum* make reasonably compact plants for the front of a sunny border, rock garden or containers on patios, and will survive for a second or third year after sowing, given good drainage and a dry summer. However, they are easily raised from seed and can be treated as annuals.

D. tatsienense Selections

Another dwarf-flowering species for the front of the border is *D. tatsienense* from western China (specifically, northern Yunnan and western Sichuan). An inhabitant of grassy slopes and alpine meadows, *D. tatsienense* is apparently more restricted in distribution than dwarf forms of *D. grandiflorum* and differs in possessing

ABOVE: **Figure 3.19c.** 'Snow White'.

a longer spur in proportion to the size of the other sepals. *D. tatsienense* has heavily dissected foliage and bears compound racemes of two or three branching spikes. Although a perennial that is intolerant of wet winter conditions, this species will survive in well-drained tubs or when the winter is dry, but it is usually grown as an annual. Selections that can be grown include '**Skylights**', which provides bushy plants with long-spurred flowers in deep blue, light blue and pink, or '**Mediterranean Seas**', in a similar mixture of colours.

LEFT: **Figure 3.20a.**
D. requienii growing in the garden border.

Species and Species Hybrids

Relatively few species delphiniums are offered for sale commercially. While most are selections rather than true wild material, it is possible to obtain unselected or wild-gathered seed.

D. requienii

This biennial species, first described by Augustin de Candolle in 1815, normally grows in a limited number of Mediterranean regions, namely the Îles

BELOW: **Figure 3.20b.** Flowers of *D. requienii* are small and dainty.

d'Hyères (off the south coast of France), Corsica and possibly Sardinia. A lush green plant at all stages of growth, seedlings from a May sowing grow rapidly but usually show no signs of a flowering stem in their first season. The size reached before winter depends on age and site, and their ability to survive in southern England seems to depend on the amount of snow cover. Snow seems to break plant tissues of this species, allowing rotting to commence. Growing a large number of seedlings gives one a chance that some will over-winter successfully and in their second year that these plants will produce a flowering stem in late May. Flowers open in June and flowering will continue with a succession of laterals until late August. The main stem may be in excess of 1.3 metres (51 inches) in height, and individual plants, with their numerous laterals, give a massive 'haze' of colour. The individual flowers are small, with a dainty appearance reminiscent of small orchids (see **Figures 3.20a and b**).

The combination of grey-green sepals flushed with pink and the large number of stamens with their bright purple anthers is extremely attractive to bees and other insects. We have grown *D. requienii* since 1979 and every year countless self-sown seedlings have appeared from the vast numbers of seeds produced by the plants. We treat these seedlings as 'weeds', leaving only a few to flower in successive summers. After flowering all plants die; they are biennial, not perennial as suggested by some authorities.

D. venulosum

It is well worth looking for this truly annual delphinium, which comes from the eastern Mediterranean and is commercially available under the name '**Rhapsody in Blue**'. Sown in late March, tall bushy plants with multiply branched stems up to 1 metre (39 inches) in height carry numerous small florets in deep purplish blue. In spite of the size of the florets, the overall effect is a mass of colour in late summer over a long period as the plants continue to branch. These annual plants also produce a prolific quantity of seed.

Delphiniums with Red Flowers

D. cardinale

The two delphiniums with truly red flowers, *D. cardinale* and *D. nudicaule*, are both natives of California. They can be grown successfully elsewhere, although they need careful siting to be perennial in the garden. *D. cardinale* is a striking, tall plant from the coastal ranges of California between San Benito County southwards to Santa Barbara and into lower California. Living on well-drained, thin soils of coastal hills and the rocky beds of canyon floors, these delphiniums are scattered through the sparse cover of shrubs (60–90 centimetres/24–35 inches high), termed *chaparral*, giving a blaze of colour during the flowering period between early May and July. The flowering stems, generally 0.9–1.8 metres (35–71 inches) in height but often as tall as 2.4 metres (94 inches), bear a central spike with many side branches (compound raceme) on which are scarlet florets. These florets have scarlet sepals, yellow upper petals overlaid with red, red lower petals with yellow hairs, and very prominent yellow anthers bearing copious quantities of pollen (see **Figure 2.7k**).

Plants of *D. cardinale* rely on winter rainfall to stimulate spring growth, after which they flower and then become dormant during the remaining months. In times of drought, growth is poor and flowers are few, which is probably why David Douglas, collecting near Santa Barbara in 1831, failed to notice this particular delphinium.

The intensity of colour found in the wild forms varies from bright scarlet through paler shades to orange and yellow. The yellow variants are rare but have been noted in the wild, especially by Gustav Mehlquist in 1937 near the present city of Lompoc in south-western Santa Barbara County. This variation in colour has been the basis of selection in the forms of *D. cardinale* offered by some seed companies such as the **'Butterfly'** series and the **'Beverley Hills'** series, the salmon-coloured flowers in the latter being very interesting (see **Figure 3.21a**).

Consideration of the habitat of *D. cardinale* should help gardeners to grow this species successfully. First, these plants grow through short shrubs that give support to the main stem, which has a surprisingly fragile attachment to the root. In our gardens, these stems are very susceptible to wind damage and must be given support. Second, dormancy following flowering needs to be maintained as long as possible, since rainfall will stimulate the appearance of basal leaves. This can be during December, and these growths can be damaged by severe frosts.

D. nudicaule

The smaller of the two red delphiniums, *D. nudicaule*, is normally only 25–50 centimetres (10–20 inches) tall, although variants up to 1.25 metres (49 inches) have been recorded from some habitats. *D. nudicaule* occurs over a wide area of California, from the mid-state counties of Monterey and Mariposa northwards to the four western border counties of Oregon, being found in coastal regions and at up to 2,000 metres (6,600 feet) in the mountains. This is a considerable area some 640 kilometres long by 240 kilometres wide (400 by 150 miles) and with a very variable environment. Thus *D. nudicaule* grows in thickets, deciduous woodlands, *chaparral* and open rocky slopes. These often have a north-westerly aspect, with pockets of humus collected between the rocks offering a wet root run. Flowering earlier than *D. cardinale*, *D. nudicaule* is in flower from mid-March to late June.

Collected by Douglas in 1831, the plant was offered for sale in Britain around 1871 by William Thompson of Ipswich, and later was listed by the German seedsmen Haage & Schmidt, by French seedsmen, and in Britain by Kelway and Sons. These firms offered a variety of colour forms, from brilliant scarlet to orange-yellow and yellow. However, interest in *D. nudicaule* waned until recently, when an orange-red selection, **'Laurin'**, and a more scarlet selection, **'Red Fox'**, have become available. Although not reliably hardy in the United Kingdom, it is so easy to grow from seed that it deserves a

return to popularity. Grown as a group of plants in a rock garden or in containers, we have found them to be good survivors with quite large plants produced over the subsequent years.

D. x ruysii 'Pink Sensation'

D. nudicaule has been used in a number of attempts to produce red-flowered *elatum* hybrids. In the early years of the 20th century, the Dutch nurseryman Ruys attempted to cross *D. elatum* with *D. nudicaule*. However, the difference in chromosome number (32 in the former, 16 in the latter) led to failure. By chance, a natural mutation – an increase in ploidy – occurred among a large batch of *D. nudicaule* seedlings, and cross pollination by *D. elatum* plants in the vicinity led to one purple seedling that appeared to be of *elatum* type. Seedlings from this plant eventually led to the delphinium **'Pink Sensation'**, which was registered in 1937. This plant, with a branching habit and single pink flowers, eventually became popular, as it was similar to belladonna delphiniums in habit. Unfortunately it has been grouped by many as a belladonna, which it certainly is not. It is still available today, but so long after its introduction, we wonder if it remains true to the original parent plant.

Delphinium 'University Hybrids'

Much later, another Dutchman, Dr. Robert Legro, was more successful in producing red *elatum* hybrids. Working at the Agricultural University at Wageningen, the first attempts were made, using plants of either *D. nudicaule* or *D. cardinale* in which the chromosome number had been doubled. Crossing these with *D. elatum* hybrids failed because the seeds obtained either did not germinate, or gave unsatisfactory seedlings. The breakthrough came when Legro first crossed *D. nudicaule* with *D. cardinale* as diploids – a species cross – and then treated the offspring with colchicine to effect a doubling of their chromosome number. The tetraploids derived in this way were then crossed with garden *elatum* hybrids to give the forerunners of the University Hybrids (see chapter 4).

After many years of work, the 'University Hybrid' selections were spectacular, with *elatum*-like foliage but flowers in fiery red, orange and even crimson shades. However, unsatisfactory features of the flowers, such as very ugly spurred petals draped across the face of florets, or flowerless 'rat-tails' at the top of the spike, proved very persistent faults. When selected plants were grown in trial plantings at the RHS Garden at Wisley, few met the standards required for commercial success as garden plants, being difficult to propagate, poor survivors in outside environments and very prone to mildew.

Fortunately, a test of the suitability of 'University Hybrid' selections for micropropagation proved successful. The first cultivar maintained in tissue culture was named **'Princess Caroline'**, and when grown under glass for the cut-flower trade in the Netherlands the pink blooms were a huge success with florists. 'Princess Caroline' and a small number of other 'University Hybrid' cultivars continue to be propagated in their millions from tissue culture for the cut-flower industry all over the world. Some plants of these cultivars are also marketed for use as garden plants, usually being supplied as mini-plants in small plugs. Apart from 'Princess Caroline', cultivars available include the deeper red **'Red Caroline' (Figure 3.21b)**, **'Red Rocket'** and **'Coral Sunset'**, the latter having a softer, peach-tinted colour. These are sold for use in the herbaceous border, but it should be remembered that the red delphiniums in their ancestry demand well-drained conditions.

BELOW: **Figure 3.21b.** '**Red Caroline'**, a 'University Hybrid' cultivar.

Delphiniums with Yellow Flowers

D. semibarbatum

Just as spectacular as the red delphiniums from California, yellow delphiniums are found across a large area of central Asia, where they grow in semi-desert regions such as the rolling hills of Afghanistan and Iran. This delphinium is *D. semibarbatum*, formerly known as, and often still called, *D. zalil*. The two names exist because a Dr James Aitchison, a British civil servant based in south-east Asia, sent seeds of this golden-flowered delphinium to the Botanic Gardens at Kew. There in 1885 it was described and named as *D. zalil* Aitch. & Hemsl., but it was later decided that it is the same species described as *D. semibarbatum* by Bienert in 1867.

Seed of *D. semibarbatum* is offered for sale commercially, and some suppliers indicate that their supply has improved germination characteristics compared to those typical of the species. It is a plant with a tuberous root, and after flowering it remains dormant until winter moisture activates root growth. Following the production of much-divided leaves, the flowering stem then grows to 80 centimetres (31 inches) in height, with a column of close-packed florets. These tend to develop together and open to give flowers composed of sulphur-yellow sepals and petals, with the upper petals being marked with orange (see **Figure 3.21c**). There is some variation in the colour of flowers from different sources of seed, and the yellow sepals may be rather pale. The numerous laterals continue the display and, in a good summer, plants can produce large amounts of seed before lapsing into dormancy. We find that plants of *D. semibarbatum* frequently do not reach maturity in their first summer; leaves go yellow and die, and the plants quickly lapse into dormancy. They will reappear in the second year, so long as conditions allow the cycle of dormancy and early growth after winter rain. *D. semibarbatum* makes a fine cut flower, and merits space in the garden, especially at the base of a sunny wall, or as a specimen plant.

ABOVE: **Figure 3.21c.** *D. semibarbatum.*

LEFT: **Figure 3.21d.**
Fully double rosy-pink
flowers of an annual
larkspur (*Consolida*).

Annual Larkspurs (Consolida)

The flowers that most gardeners call 'larkspurs' are annuals that belong to the genus *Consolida*. Although these annuals with simple branched stems were separated from delphiniums in the early 19th century, this distinction is not always made in seed catalogues, leading to some confusion.

The exact parentage of modern types of garden larkspurs is not easy to determine but they are thought to be derived from the rocket larkspur, *C. ambigua*, and the branching or field larkspur, *C. regalis*, both European species. *C. ambigua* produces a dense raceme of single florets in shades of pink to deep blue, and white flowers can also be found. *C. orientalis*, with deep violet-purple flowers, is a rather similar larkspur, which was originally called *D. ajacis* L., a name now rejected by botanists but which may still be found in seed catalogues. *C. regalis* is a branching plant bearing short racemes of a few florets with blue sepals and a lilac petal. Available selections of this plant with single flowers are **'Blue Cloud'**, **'White Cloud'** and, as a mixture, **'Cloudy Skies'**.

C. ambigua gave rise to the **'Hyacinth'** or **'Rocket'** larkspurs that were very popular before World War II. They had single spikes of double flowers in light and dark blue, pink and white, and grew to about 90 centimetres (35 inches), while there were also dwarf forms reaching 30 centimetres (12 inches). These larkspurs were produced by German seedsmen but were generally lost during the war, except for a few lines that survived in France and the Netherlands. Hyacinth larkspurs have been redeveloped to give more weather-resistant types, and are earlier flowering than those derived from *C. regalis*.

In its natural state a single-flowered branching larkspur, *C. regalis* was also developed to give double-flowered forms, called **'Stock-flowered larkspurs'**, which were still loosely branching but had relatively short stems. In the 1930s selection from these gave rise to the **'Giant Imperial'** types, with a compact and upright habit and branches down to the base bearing improved numbers of secondary spikes. These became popular as garden plants and for cut flowers, with names such as **'Carmine King'** and **'Dazzler'** and available in white plus six other colours. Further development in the United States led to new lines known as the **'Regal'** and **'Supreme'** types. Today, further reselection of the 'Giant Imperial' lines include the **'Sublime'** series, with solid stems and fully double flowers in all colours and shades (**Figure 3.21d**), and the **'Exquisite'** series, using old names such as 'Carmine King' and **'Rosequeen'**. The demands of the cut-flower trade have led to the **'Sidney'** series, which have upright flowers in shades of pink, purple, rose and white, coupled with uniform growth and rapid flowering in the glasshouse in 14 weeks from seed.

There are therefore a number of different series of larkspurs that are well worth growing, either for filling areas with annuals, in the perennial border, or in rows for cut flowers. A useful feature of these larkspurs is that they readily provide clear pink and brilliant red flowers to interplant with delphiniums. One enterprising farmer in the Vale of Evesham, Worcestershire, has devoted 16 acres to growing larkspurs in pink, purple, lavender and ivory for the production of 'petal confetti'. From this area he produces annually approximately 11,300 litres (20,000 pints) of petals, which are harvested, dried, packaged and marketed as a completely natural biodegradable product to replace less ecologically friendly paper confetti.

4. Breeding Delphiniums

The quality of named delphinium cultivars, particularly of their flowers, tends to deteriorate over time. Unless rigorous selection is applied to the plants used in vegetative propagation, small changes in plant form (somatic mutations) become regular features of the cultivar stock. For this reason, it is very doubtful if historic delphiniums are true descendants of the original cultivar, although some devoted gardeners may have faithfully maintained their old named delphiniums. The life span of named delphinium cultivars is also limited by disease. There is therefore a continual need for the breeding of new plants that can serve as replacements for those in decline, and widen the range of colours and plant form available.

The breeding of new delphiniums begins with the raising of plants from seed obtained from cultivars selected for some particular qualities. Many such desirable characteristics in cultivated delphiniums are genetically recessive and thus are readily lost in random pollination. For example, a single flower may replace the semi-double flower. Plant breeders therefore make hand-crosses between their plants in order to retain the desirable features. The second aspect of such breeding programmes is the selection of the best plants from among the seedlings obtained since these F1 hybrids do not necessarily show the characteristics being sought. The process of making a hand-cross is not difficult, and there is much enjoyment to be gained from raising your own new delphiniums.

The Basis of Delphinium Hybridization

Some understanding of the basis of hybridization is required to reduce the time spent on making hand-crosses likely to yield poor plants. Characteristics of a plant, for example flower colour, are each associated with one or more genes carried on the chromosomes residing within the cell nucleus. This information passes from parents to offspring during hybridization. The nucleus of a somatic cell contains two sets of chromosomes, one set derived from each parent, and is said to be diploid. Most *Delphinium* species are diploid, with two sets of 8 chromosomes (2n=16) but cultivated garden *elatum* hybrids are tetraploid, possessing four sets of eight chromosomes (2n=32), two sets coming from each parent. The origins of this change in ploidy are unclear, and though numerous attempts have been made to trace the evolution of our garden delphiniums, the problem has not been resolved. The tetraploid condition of the garden *elatum* hybrid is the reason that crosses with species delphiniums fail to give either viable seed or fertile offspring.

During plant growth, cell division ensures that each daughter cell receives copies of all the chromosome sets. However, reproductive cells (gametes), either ovules or pollen grains, are produced by a special division sequence known as reduction division, by which gametes receive only one copy of each chromosome set. Thus gametes contain half the original number of chromosomes. After fertilization, when chromosomes from a pollen grain are merged with those in an ovule, the full complement of chromosomes is restored.

The nature of genetic material gives rise to multiple forms (alleles) of any one gene and the form seen in the offspring will depend on whether the individual characteristics that chance has selected are dominant or recessive. The chances of recessive characters appearing in the offspring are reduced if the plant is tetraploid. The simplest way to understand this situation is to look at the inheritance of a single characteristic.

Since flower colour will be important for many gardeners trying to produce new plants, we will consider this character to be determined by one gene. We can represent the two forms of the gene as **'coloured'** (W) and **'white'** (w) with 'coloured' being dominant to 'white'. In a diploid, the combination of genes on the parental chromosomes can be WW, Ww, wW, or ww. Because W is dominant, every allele in which it appears will be coloured, so only the combination ww will produce a white flower. In a cross between two coloured parents, both being Ww, we can illustrate the situation as follows:

Ww	x	Ww	parents both coloured
W w		W w	ovules and pollen grains
WW Ww		Ww ww	offspring

The result will be 3 pairings corresponding to coloured flowers and 1 to white, so that 75 per cent of the offspring will be coloured and 25 per cent white.

However, when the plants are tetraploid, the chance that the recessive character will appear is considerably reduced, as in the following example. Again taking two coloured parents, but both carrying recessive white genes (WWww):

WWww	x	WWww		parents
WW Ww (x4) ww		WW Ww (x4) ww		ovules/pollen
WWWW or WWWw or WWww or Wwww or wwww				offspring
1	8	18	8	1

Now, only the set wwww of the 36 possible combinations will yield plants with white flowers, which is just 2.8 per cent of the total offspring.

This ratio can be increased by using two coloured plants that are both Wwww, of which 25 per cent of the offspring will be

white, or by using one coloured parent, Wwww, with one white parent, wwww, of which 50 per cent of the offspring should be white. Of course, a sufficient number of seedlings need to be grown to flowering to verify the statistics. These statistics emphasize how a dominant undesirable characteristic, such as 'single' flowers, can quickly cause the deterioration of delphiniums raised from open-pollinated seed. Clearly it would be naive to think that any characteristic is controlled only by one gene, but the gene complex controlling sepal colour does seem to obey these rules. Within the colours of delphinium sepals, there would appear to be a hierarchical dominance – in the order purple, blue, lavender, pink, and white – and where there is no clear dominance, pastel blue with a heavy lavender flush is seen.

The colour of the petals (eye) is less easy to predict, but black appears to be dominant to brown, and both to white. Often the petals bear lines of the colour seen in the sepals and this is especially common in white-eye petals.

We have not noticed any difference in results from reciprocal crosses, such as pollen from a white parent onto a coloured parent and vice versa. This is in accordance with the rules set out by the father of genetics, Gregor Mendel. However some characteristics might be inherited in a non-Mendelian way due to cytoplasmic inheritance; those influenced by mitochondrial or chloroplast DNA to give an example.

Breeding Delphiniums with Cream Flowers

One interesting example where it does seem possible to readily predict the results of hybridization involves the production of 'cream' delphiniums. These possess florets with sepals that may vary in the depth of their creamy-yellow colour, but which are clearly different to white. The eye or petals may be yellow when they enhance the 'cream' effect, brown or black. Cream-coloured florets are closely linked with the appearance of the plant, which possesses bronzed and shiny leaves and a poor growth habit. Such seedlings can be readily identified even when quite young, and often fail to survive. This cream colour is recessive relative to all other colours, including white. In order to obtain the highest possible yield of cream offspring – 50 per cent – a coloured seed parent of a cross must possess only one 'colour' gene to three 'cream' (Cccc) while the other parent is a cream (cccc). This is one instance where the cross generally can only be made in one direction; namely pollen from a cream is used on a coloured seed parent. The problem here seems to be incompatibility, as the stigma of a cream plant seems to be unable to accept pollen, although we have not fully explored this. One might ask whether it is possible to cross one cream plant with another cream to obtain 100 per cent cream offspring. We have managed to get cream hybrids in this way only once. This happened the first time that we attempted such a cross some 35 years ago using two cream sister seedlings. At the time we did not realize the significance of this result, and we have never been able to duplicate it.

Desirable Characteristics for Garden Delphiniums

Apart from colour, it is not easy to deal with most flower characters in such a clear-cut way. As a general rule, most desirable features seem to be recessive, such as the increased number of sepals in a semi-double flower. The florets must be of good form – preferably flat and open rather than cupped or hooded – and the spur belonging to the petals should not be exposed across the face of the sepals but buried as far as possible. The colour should develop under all weather conditions; many blue flowers show considerable pink coloration in the centre during hot weather if flower development has been very rapid. Flowers must not fade in strong sunlight such that the lowest florets are pale and dingy when compared to those higher up the spike. The darker pink shades are very prone to this defect.

Other characteristics that we call desirable, such as the height of the plant and the form of the spike, are clearly the result of the interaction of a number of genes. We can select for plants showing thin sturdy stems, generous leaf size, vigorous crown development, and whether the time of peak flowering is early or late in the season, but most of these characteristics are not easy to predict. Low susceptibility to powdery mildew is also an important characteristic, and one that appears to be related to colour, since purples and deep lavenders are generally the first plants to be infected with the fungus.

When choosing parents for crosses, a delphinium breeder relies to a certain extent on information available about the parentage of the selected cultivar or his own seedlings; a record book of all crosses grown is a real necessity. Some information about named cultivars can be obtained from the International Delphinium Register, which is compiled by the Royal Horticultural Society at the Wisley Gardens. However, this is not always very helpful since many cultivars are registered as 'parentage unknown' or 'cross with an unnamed seedling'. One need not despair, as growers who become addicted to delphinium breeding (or that of any other plant) will soon build up a library of information, especially if their breeding work concentrates on a few specific characteristics. We have kept records over a very long time and know, for example, which seed parent to use in the production of cream seedlings. Thus we would use such pink cultivars as 'Royal Flush' or 'Rosemary Brock', but not 'Cherub' or 'Summerfield Miranda'; white cultivars such as 'Olive Poppleton' or 'Sandpiper'; amethyst cultivar 'Gordon Forsyth', or the pale violet 'Emily Hawkins'.

True-breeding Colour Lines

Although the need for seed lines producing uniform plants of high quality is very important for today's markets, neither we, nor most amateurs, can work on the scale of line breeding used by Reinelt to produce the Pacific Hybrids. The development of individual colour lines involved selecting the best two plants of a colour, hand-crossing all the florets to create the F1 generation, and growing all the resulting seedlings, say between 500 and 1,000. The best two F1 seedlings were then selfed – that is, hand-crossed within the plant – and around 2,000–5,000 seedlings grown. Once again the best two were selected and, this time, crossed with each other, to be followed in the third generation by the selection of the two best and selfing again. Reinelt continued this process for 25 generations. Having obtained a satisfactory colour line, it then needed to be carefully maintained for commercial seed production.

Reinelt's description of the methods used at Capitola after 1945 indicates that 5,000 seedlings of each colour line (10,000 for the most popular lines) were grown annually from seed sown in August. Seedlings were planted out in October and bloomed during April and May. Individual colour lines were grown in blocks to reduce any interbreeding. Accounts by visitors to his nursery indicate that inferior plants were eliminated at flowering time. After the seed crop had been harvested, the plants were ploughed under and none were retained.

A rigorous selection procedure was adopted to obtain the seed of each colour line needed for the following year's crop. This seed was collected from about six plants that had been assessed as being the best in the block. In alternate years, these selected plants would either be inter-crossed to obtain the seed, or allowed to set seed naturally, this procedure being adopted to avoid the introduction of undesirable recessive traits. Over time the quality of the flowers improved with respect to colour clarity, flower size and bloom structure. The effort required, and the amount of land that had to be used, were phenomenal.

On a considerably smaller scale, we use a mix of line breeding for a steady improvement of colour, combined with out-crossing with other seedling lines to maintain the vigour of our plants.

'Rosemary Brock', a cultivar introduced in 1985 and which we consider to be one of our successes, was the result of this approach. In 1971 the cross 'Cinderella' (heliotrope) x 'Turkish Delight' (pink) gave a mixture of seedlings in violets, pale blue/lavenders, and a few creams. Back-crossing to 'Turkish Delight' regained some pale pink seedlings, and the colour was improved by inter-crossing between them and also crossing with some deeper-pink seedlings obtained from the cross 'Turkish Delight' x 'Strawberry Fair' (deep pink). The resulting plants had good, flat florets with neat eyes, but were not very vigorous, and we lost a lot of plants over the winter. At the same time, there were a few very pale pink flowers in a batch of seedlings from another cross between the lavenders 'Emily Hawkins' and 'Gillian Dallas'. These would normally have been discarded on the basis of colour, but they were very tall and vigorous, one regularly producing a large number of spikes. Crossed to our best deep-pink seedling from the previous batch, this plant gave us 75 per cent pinks, in shades from very pale to very deep, and 25 per cent creams. We called this seed line 'Strawberries and Cream', and selected the best pink for propagation. Named 'Rosemary Brock', for a neighbour who allowed us to use her garden for our flowers, this flower with a pyramidal spike, flat mid-pink florets and a brown eye with golden hairs has been one to be proud of.

Breeding Delphiniums with Red Flowers

Although we call our flowers pink, to many people they do not justify this term, and they are seen as pale mauve. This colour is due to the anthocyanin pigment involved in our flowers, which results in the bluish colour of many pink flowers. The brilliance of the colour in the wild red delphiniums, *D. cardinale* and *D. nudicaule*, has always fascinated plantsmen. The desire to introduce this colour into *elatum* garden hybrids has occupied the minds of many hybridizers in the United States and

Europe. The late Dr A A Samuelson, talking of *D. cardinale*, said: 'Youth has grown old in the pursuit of its intriguing colour'. 'Pink Sensation', the single-flowered *nudicaule–elatum* hybrid raised by chance after many years of fruitless effort by Ruys, and registered in 1937, has not been developed further.

The length of time and energy required in any attempt to introduce a specific characteristic (such as red flowers) from a species into garden hybrids – and without undesirable characteristics such as single florets, short spike length and poor root systems – can be seen in the development of the University Hybrids. Commencing in 1953 at the University of Wageningen, Dr Robert Legro started a programme designed to investigate hybridization in delphinium species with the goal of introducing red and yellow flower colour into cultivated *elatum* hybrids. Aware that differences in chromosome number between species and garden hybrids led to non-viable seeds, Bob looked in detail at the effects of colchicine treatment on *D. nudicaule, cardinale* and *semibarbatum* in order to create tetraploid individuals. He found that whereas *D. nudicaule* became tetraploid rather easily, *D. cardinale* and *D. semibarbatum* were less inclined to do so. Crossing *elatum hybrids* (1,402 florets) with pollen from tetraploid *D. nudicaule* yielded 6 seeds, though all failed to germinate. However, in the opposite cross, tetraploid *D. nudicaule* x *elatum* hybrid (277 florets), 55 seeds were obtained, of which 8 gave rise to purplish-flowered seedlings. These seedlings were selfed in their second year to yield 1,200 seeds, from which 700 plants were raised and flowered. The seedlings gave a marvellous mix of colours from pale orange and rose to pink and dark violet, but all florets were single. Rather similar results were obtained using a Pacific Hybrid 'Astolat' cultivar as the pollen source, since seedlings obtained were all single. The orange colour appeared to be very strongly linked to the single form of floret.

Using *D. cardinale*, very few tetraploid plants could be obtained, and when pollen from these few plants was crossed onto *elatum* hybrids, the 94 seeds obtained failed to germinate. This was depressing since *D. cardinale* would seem to be a better starting point for hybridization, for not only are they a bright scarlet, but they are tall plants with a root system more fibrous in texture than the tuberous *nudicaule*.

The really important step forward was the decision to cross *D. nudicaule* with *D. cardinale* to give diploid species hybrids. From 304 seeds, 253 seedlings were obtained. These were treated with colchicine in an attempt to produce tetraploids, allotetraploids with 16 chromosomes from *D. nudicaule* and 16 chromosomes from *D. cardinale*. Following this treatment, 20 self-fertile plants were obtained, which were intermediate in type with single orange flowers. Once again, crosses using pollen from these *nudicaule–cardinale* flowers on a number of different *elatum* cultivars gave a few non-viable seeds. The reciprocal cross using nudicaule–cardinale as the seed parent and *elatum* hybrid pollen was, however, successful, giving a large number of fertile seeds. The seedlings (F1) obtained had 'single' flowers that varied in colour from lilac to royal purple, rosy purple to dark violet, depending on the cultivar used to provide the pollen. Although not all these F1 seedlings were fertile, sufficient seedlings were crossed (F2), and these gave rise to some 2,400 plants. The majority of these plants were pale purple to dark violet and with single, semi-double and double florets. Around 60 plants were orange, pink or red, with a floret size around 2.5–5 centimetres (1–2 inches), and some of these were semi-double!

The desired combination of colour and semi-double florets had been achieved, but other problems arise in this kind of breeding programme. As an example, an apricot-orange seedling with semi-double florets and an *elatum*-like appearance, although with only 20 florets in the spike, was completely self-sterile, but fertile when crossed with siblings. Self-sterility occurred in many of the desirable 'red' plants, but the work was continued by inter-crossing the best carmine and rosy-carmine plants. It proved difficult to maintain semi-double flowers on a good *elatum*-shaped spike, however, since undesirable characteristics such as tiny spikes with numerous long laterals and very poor root systems appeared to be dominant. Additionally, it should be realized that working to produce this F3 generation involved hand-pollinating over 4,000 florets.

This patient and prolonged work led to some material, which received the name of 'University Hybrids', being released to four Dutch growers at the end of 1963; it was hoped that commercial introductions would be made by 1967 (see **Figure 4.1**).

At the same time, Blackmore & Langdon had commenced a similar breeding programme to obtain red-flowered *elatum* cultivars, but they reported that although some lovely plants arose, there were problems. The plants had good-sized semi-double florets borne on spikes of 60–90 centimetres (24–35 inches), but they were very susceptible to

BELOW: **Figure 4.1.** '**University Hybrid**' delphiniums growing in a greenhouse at the University of Wageningen, 1977.

mildew and of generally poor root configuration. In an attempt to overcome these problems, Dr Brian Langdon used pollen from a batch of seedlings grown from crosses involving *D. cardinale* only, which had been sent to him by Professor Gustav Mehlquist, working in Connecticut. Although they did not help with the mildew problem, better root systems were obtained. We remember seeing these lovely flowers in a wide spectrum of red colours in the greenhouses at Stanton Nurseries in 1969. In the end it was considered that they would not be commercially viable, and sadly the project was abandoned around 1972.

Although Legro continued his patient work for some 25 years, the very low germination rates of seed, mildew susceptibility and the failure to propagate these plants vegetatively (due to lack of shoots for cutting material) still remained problematic for the best bright reds. By 1981 the University of Wageningen had terminated the research work and Legro moved to the Royal Horticultural Society Gardens at Wisley to continue his work (see **Figure 4.2**). A large number of seedlings were grown, and some selections made among those that were considered the best red shades. These were registered as **'Red Start'** and **'Red Cardinal'**. Personally we found the salmon shades to be equally attractive as flowers. However, although planted outside in the Trial grounds, the plants did not survive and were considered to be commercially non-viable. So after many years of work red delphiniums that will survive under garden conditions remain elusive.

The technique of micropropagation offered a chance of producing a large number of plants without regard to the rooting system of the plant. The technique was applied successfully to one rather poor 'University Hybrid' plant with rather small, pale-pink florets. This plant, named 'Princess Caroline', is now grown in quantities of millions under glass for the cut-flower industry.

LEFT: **Figure 4.2.**
Several florets of a
'University Hybrid'
delphinium growing in a
greenhouse at the Royal
Horticultural Society
Gardens, Wisley, 1988.

Part 2: GROWING DELPHINIUMS

5. Delphiniums in the Garden

Flowers seen in a garden, pictures in a book, a programme on television, or a vase of flowers may perhaps have first stirred an interest in delphiniums, but it is only by growing the plants ourselves that we fully appreciate their beauty. In this chapter we consider some ways to do this, looking first at the space requirements of the plants, and then at where we can place them in our surroundings, whether that means a garden or just a window box. There is a delphinium of a size to suit most situations, and we have seen in the earlier chapters that there are also flowers in many different colours to choose from. A wide range of flowering times from spring to late autumn can also be organized, either by selecting the appropriate type of delphinium or by manipulating the growing cycle of the plants. Technical details about cultivation are in the following chapters.

Plant Size

The width of the foliage and how far the roots spread in the soil determine the space needed for a delphinium to grow well, and the appropriate plant spacing when several are planted as a group.

The smallest delphiniums widely available are the various seed selections of *Delphinium grandiflorum* for blue or white flowers and *D. nudicaule* for red flowers. When flowering, these are bushy little plants with small leaves, and are typically less than 20 centimetres across by 50 centimetres tall (8 by 20 inches).

Next in the size range are dwarf delphiniums from seed selections of the Elatum group, such as 'Magic Fountains'. These have relatively large leaves on long stalks with short blooms of conventional delphinium style, and an individual plant when in flower would typically be 30–40 centimetres across by 60–90 centimetres tall (12–16 inches by 24–35 inches).

The largest plants are those of the Elatum and Belladonna groups. Whatever the height of the plants when in flower, the foliage of mature plants with several stems would typically have a spread of 60–80 centimetres (24–31 inches), while the roots spread beyond the leaf canopy and occupy an area up to 90 centimetres (35 inches) across. It is useful to note that young plants with only one stem occupy a much smaller area, typically only 30 centimetres (12 inches) across.

Planting Site Considerations

For best results, most delphiniums need an open site providing good light, good air circulation around the foliage and free-draining soil.

In Britain, a site in full sunshine is good, although in strong sunshine the colour of flowers can be bleached and blooms dehydrated if plants do not have adequate water at the root. This scorching can be avoided if plants are located where there is shade during the hottest part of the day. There is a downside to shade, however, because it usually means there are buildings or trees nearby, and this causes delphiniums to stretch upwards towards the light and become abnormally tall. Planting delphiniums under the canopy of a tree is definitely not recommended, as tree roots normally take every drop of water available. Note that tree-root competition for water and nutrients often extends a long way from trees.

Another aspect of planting sites that should be thought about is the degree of exposure to strong winds. It is not a case of changing the place where you live just to suit the flowers, but more one of finding the most favourable spots in your given situation. One point to remember is that wind blowing around a house can create a whirlwind effect near the corners, so they are places to avoid. Another is that delphiniums should not be planted close to high garden walls, fences or hedges, however nice they may look against such a background. Wind blowing directly on the wall reflects back from it and takes the delphiniums with it. Hedges are generally better than solid fences as windbreaks because they reduce the wind speed, but their disadvantage is that they have roots that compete with your plants in the nearby flower bed.

Delphiniums in Flowerbeds

When you have a special interest in delphiniums, as we do, it is natural that there will be many of them in your garden. We have had sufficient space to use the delphiniums in combination with a varied selection of other plants, and we use a variety of approaches to placing them so that all the plants contribute to a colourful display of flowers.

We have always been enthusiasts for the typical English herbaceous border, which is an excellent setting for delphiniums because they can be grown with a wide variety of other perennials that provide colour from June to October. Our favourite perennials include peonies, lupins, several types of salvia, anthemis, border phlox, heleniums, rudbeckias, *Geranium psilostemum* and so on. We generally organize the planting on the basis of plant height rather than try to achieve particular combinations of colour or plant texture. However, the plants somehow manage to achieve such effects. Experience over many years confirms that it is best to have delphiniums mainly at the side of the bed adjacent to a grass path, as it is then easy to attend to staking and tying them up. The flowers there provide a background to the other perennials. We prefer borders that are curved and of varying width, and use a few tall delphiniums at the front or in the middle to provide focal points. For these mixed borders, we used either named delphiniums or reliable selected seedlings that can be left in place on a semi-permanent basis (see **Figure 5.1**).

ABOVE: **Figure 5.1.** A colourful display of flowers with a background of delphiniums.

LEFT: **Figure 5.2.**
Delphiniums viewed across
creamy anthemis and
purple salvias.

A second approach to using mature delphiniums is a bed in which they are the principal components of the planting. Such a flowerbed could be a small, round island bed, large enough for perhaps 3–5 delphiniums, which would make a striking feature, or it could be a larger area with many delphiniums. We use plantings of this type to accommodate the delphiniums selected from the large numbers of seedlings that we grow each year in our efforts to breed interesting new cultivars. As a consequence many of the delphiniums are replaced annually, with the new plants being moved into position in March or April. Dusky-pink blooms stick up like sore thumbs in a bed of blue flowers, so it is worth taking some care over the plants used. We now restrict one bed to dusky pinks and cream-flowered plants, another to blues with a few whites, while the purple and violet shades go with the white flowers. An advantage of this is that the beds of delphiniums may then merge into the rest of the planting in the garden. Our bed of pink and cream delphiniums, for example, looked splendid when viewed across the patches of creamy-yellow anthemis and purple salvias in the adjacent border (see **Figure 5.2**).

The major problem with such a bed of delphiniums arises once the flowers are over. A flowerbed full of towering seed heads looks attractive to bullfinches, but not to us. We need to collect seed, but obviously it is usually best to cut off the seed heads. This still leaves an unsightly collection of plants and their supporting canes, so inter-planting with other flowers is sensible. Dahlias are a good choice for this, as cuttings are planted out in late May, either round the edges of the bed or in gaps in the middle that provide access for staking and tying up the delphiniums. The dahlias grow quickly and begin to flower as the delphiniums finish. We use tall dahlias of the various sorts used by exhibitors because they have such perfectly formed flowers and because the flower display continues until the plants are cut down by frost. Spray chrysanthemums can also be used in this way. In our bed of mainly dusky-pink delphiniums we have sometimes sown seed of red annual larkspur around the edge. We may even plant more delphiniums around the edge of the bed! For this we use seedlings that flower in August or September, usually either dwarf types that provide a good flower display, or various unfamiliar species.

It may seem sacrilegious to some, but delphinium seedlings grown from spring sowings (as described in chapter 7) can be used as 'bedding plants'. Our plots of ground with 100–250 seedlings, which we use to evaluate the results of hand-pollination, are not really normal 'bedding' because the blooms often grow to 1.5 metres (59 inches) or more, but they do provide a colourful display from August onwards (see **Figure 5.3**). It is possible to use tall types as bedding because young seedlings can be planted close together. A bed 5 by 1.8 metres (16 by 6 feet) would take about 50 plants. A more appropriate scheme for small and medium-sized gardens would be a bed mainly planted with dwarf delphiniums of the *D. grandiflorum* type, with a few taller plants of medium height dotted among them – groups of annual larkspur would be an excellent choice for this.

BELOW: **Figure 5.3**. Delphinium seedlings, six months old, provide colour in August or September.

Many wild delphinium species are plants that have an alpine origin, and a rock garden or scree bed can make a useful environment in which to grow them. Small delphinium species, such as *D. nudicaule*, *D. tatsienense* or *D. cashmerianum*, are useful because they come into flower in late summer and can brighten up an often rather drab feature at that time (see **Figure 5.4**).

BELOW: **Figure 5.4.** Dwarf species delphiniums give colour to a rock garden in late summer.

RIGHT: **Figure 5.5.** Delphiniums in containers provide colour outside the kitchen window.

Delphiniums in Containers

Most types of delphinium are readily grown in containers, as described in chapter 8, with the only snag being that they require regular attention to watering. The distinct advantage is that they become mobile plants that can be moved into place when they are in flower and removed when the flowers are over. This makes the plants suitable for use on a patio (**Figure 5.5**) or in conservatories (**Figure 5.6**).

Thinking first about specimen plants of a large named delphinium, for example 'Spindrift', you could grow this in a pot to have two large blooms on fairly short stems so that the total height above the base of the pot might be 1.6 metres (63 inches). The first point to remember is that the

LEFT: **Figure 5.6.** Glass shelters some perfect pot-grown delphiniums from the rain. The striking pinkish delphinium with a black eye is **'Darling Sue'**.

blooms are like sails, and a plant can be knocked down by a strong gust of wind just like a yacht capsizing. It is not enough that there is a cane in the pot supporting the plant, so it is essential to anchor the plant to the ground in some way.

Specimen plants in containers can be used to create exciting new features in a garden, or just to fill a gap in a border. A plant can be adequately anchored by inserting two stakes into the ground on either side of the pot and then attaching the cane(s) in the pot to these stakes. Hopefully, the foliage of adjacent plants will help to hide the unsightly pot and anchoring stakes.

The problem of anchoring delphiniums in containers is much greater if the pots are standing on the stone slabs of a terrace or patio. The best solution is to locate the pots near the edge of the paved area and to attach the plant support canes to stakes driven into the ground at the edge of the paving (see **Figure 5.7**). Features such as brick pillars or walling may also provide points to which ties to the plant-support cane(s) can be attached. Other smaller plants in containers can then be used to hide the pot. In a conservatory, the need to anchor the plant disappears, but is replaced by the need to ensure adequate ventilation and watering.

The problems of anchoring large delphiniums in containers disappear if one is less ambitious and accepts the delights of dwarf delphiniums. These can be used, for example, as companion plants for a patio rose in a stone container. Plants of

RIGHT: **Figure 5.7.** Paving slabs provide a standing ground at the back of a border for delphiniums growing in containers.

D. nudicaule have survived for several years in one of our patio planters, and the little red flowers are attractive companions to the flowers of the patio rose 'Anna Ford'. *D. grandiflorum* 'Summer Blues' or 'Summer Stars' are also well suited for patio containers or even for window boxes.

Ultimately it is your imagination and the availability of plants that limit the ways you can use delphiniums to brighten up your surroundings. Seed provides a way to generate the plants (as described in chapter 7), so just keep dreaming!

Delphiniums for Cutting

For many, one of the joys of having a garden is that you can wander outside, cut a rosebud, bring it indoors and enjoy it there. It is the same for dahlias and chrysanthemums, which last for many days in water. Delphiniums can also be enjoyed as cut blooms, but all too often the beautiful flowers fall to pieces after a very short time, covering the surroundings with a confetti of petals.

You may instantly object to this slur on the reputation of such beautiful flowers, especially if you have enjoyed blooms of the gentian-blue delphinium 'Volkerfrieden' from a florist or supermarket for two weeks or more. That is possible because the flowers are treated immediately after cutting with a chemical to prevent petal drop. The chemical used is toxic and is not considered safe for unrestricted use by amateur gardeners.

The natural loss of sepals and petals from untreated delphinium flowers, like fruit ripening, occurs as the result of ethylene released in the plant. This acts as a plant hormone, closing off the sap supplies to the flower components, which then fall off. The chemical treatment of cut flowers removes the ethylene.

Unfortunately, the sachets of 'cut flower food' commonly supplied with flowers purchased from florists or a supermarket have no effect on the problem of petal drop. However, they are very useful in helping to keep delphinium flowers fresh. These products usually contain sugar to feed the flowers and a sterilizing agent to prevent growth of bacteria in the vase water. Keeping the vase water fresh is crucial because delphinium blooms take up a large amount of water and soon flag or wilt if bacteria block the stem capillaries.

For exhibitors of large delphinium blooms it is common practice to fill the cavity of the hollow stem with water to help keep the flowers fresh. This is done by holding each bloom upside down, pouring water into the hollow stem and then plugging the end of the stem with a wad of cotton wool before placing it in a vase or arrangement. We no longer do this ourselves and it is definitely not necessary for blooms treated to stop petal drop. We are not sure that water in the stem cavity has much effect if a bloom stops taking up water because bacteria have blocked the capillaries in the wall of the hollow stem. We think it is more important to ensure that containers used for staging flowers are clean, and that vase water is kept fresh by adding sterilants.

Apart from their rather short vase life caused by petal drop, delphiniums are lovely for a vase in the house or for use in flower arrangements. It is also great fun to use your flowers in entries to a flower show. To get the best from your flowers, it is worth noting a few points about selecting the blooms that will be cut, and how to treat them.

- The flowers need to be as fresh as possible, so make sure the plants are grown with adequate soil moisture.
- Select young blooms with some florets that are not fully open, as these are likely to remain fresh longest.
- Cut flowers in the cooler parts of the day, either early morning or the evening, and stand them in fresh water as soon as possible.
- Cut off blooms with a long stem below the bloom – the excess stem can be cut off later. Large leaves can usually be trimmed off before cutting a bloom.
- Use a strong, sharp knife blade to cut blooms by making a cut diagonally across the stem. Secateurs are not recommended as they often crush the hollow stems of delphinium blooms.

- Stand the freshly cut flowers in a cool place in deep water for a period of several hours immediately after cutting so that they drink and become fully charged with water.
- After a bloom has been out of water for more than a few minutes, always cut a slice off the bottom of the stem before inserting it in water again. This is to ensure that the capillaries in the stem are open and able to take up water.

Delphinium blooms of even modest size pose problems in handling because they are top heavy and fragile. When cutting flowers in the garden, it is not advisable to try standing the cut blooms in a container of water, as a gust of wind is quite likely to cause them to topple over, just like delphinium plants in pots. It is far safer to lay them down gently on the grass in a shady spot for a minute or two and then carry them indoors where they can be stood in a stable container filled with water.

All types of delphinium can be used for cutting, and some types seem to have a longer vase-life than others. It is really a case of trying the flowers available in your garden and finding the ones that respond best. Alternatively, you could grow one of the types of delphinium developed specifically for commercial horticulture by raising plants from seed. *Delphinium* 'Guardian' F1, 'Clear Springs' and 'Aurora' are three seed series of this type, and each has several series that provide flowers of a particular colour. Unfortunately, it would be normal for the flowers to be chemically treated to prevent petal drop after cutting, so it is unlikely that without this treatment these types would have any greater inherent resistance to petal dropping than other garden delphiniums.

6. Cultivation of Delphiniums

While garden delphiniums are not too particular in their requirements, attention to some aspects of cultivation will repay you with a top-class performance during the flowering season and long-lived plants as part of a garden display over quite a number of years.

Soil Requirements

As a home for the growing plant, the soil must provide nutrients and an adequate supply of water without water-logging during the winter months when the plants are dormant. These requirements are best met by soils with some clay content rather than those that are largely sandy and do not retain water during dry summer months. Most soils can be improved to grow good flowers or vegetables by the use of composts, manure or fertilizers.

Soils with a neutral pH are preferable, but delphiniums will tolerate more acid soils, or alkaline clays over chalk. Shallow soils over chalk give good drainage during the winter months but require more watering during dry periods, plus the addition of magnesium (we use Epsom Salts) to avoid yellowing of the leaves during periods of rapid growth. Even sandy soils, such as the impoverished acid sands typified by natural heathland with Silver Birch (*Betula pendula*) and Scots Pine (*Pinus sylvestris*), or light sandy soils such as those at the RHS Gardens at Wisley in Surrey, can be improved by working in suitable materials. Garden compost, which in many gardens will include lawn mowings, leaves from deciduous trees and household vegetable waste, is beneficial. Remember that neither grass cuttings (if weedkillers have been used) nor moss raked from lawns (if treated with mosskiller) should be saved. The addition of stable manure, if available, will improve the compost, but this manure should be straw-based rather than sawdust, which does not break down quickly.

While a fibrous loam might be considered ideal by many gardeners, most of us cannot dictate where we have our gardens. For many in Britain, the garden soil consists of clay in varying degrees of heaviness, which is difficult to dig when wet and in very dry weather resembles crazy paving with cracks down which you can lose a small implement! These soils are also improved by the addition of fibrous material and do not need such constant watering most of the time, which is beneficial to herbaceous plants. Although it is possible to prepare lighter soils during the winter months, with heavier soils it is preferable to have completed this work before winter rains set in. Well-rotted compost should be incorporated and the soil left 'rough' to allow frost to break down the heavy lumps. With lighter soils, deep digging is not required and compost should be left in the upper levels of the soil. When it comes to planting time, it may not have been possible to prepare the site for the delphinium plants, especially within an established border. In this case, a few bucketfuls of friable compost can be dug into the planting site together with a generous dressing of fertilizer, preferably with a slow-release component such as blood, fish and bonemeal, or a good compound fertilizer such as Growmore, at 100 grams per square metre (yard).

Planting Delphiniums

The best time to plant or transplant delphiniums is during spring, when the roots are making new growth and the crowns are showing new shoots. At this time, plants quickly establish themselves in their new surroundings. New plants from cuttings, whether from commercial suppliers or your own, are unlikely to be

ABOVE: **Figure 6.1a.**
Move delphiniums with a large root ball in early spring but take care to avoid back injury.

available until early summer. These can be planted when sufficiently well-grown, but care must be taken to ensure they do not become too dry in the early weeks after planting out. If need be, plants can be moved at any time while they are in growth, providing the roots are not seriously damaged. A plant in transit, with its attendant soil ball, will be very heavy, so care should be taken when lifting (see **Figure 6.1a**). Once the season has advanced and plants have started to die down, lifting and moving them is not a good idea and should be avoided if possible. In late autumn and winter, plants are dormant and will not make any new root growth into the ground. During these weeks, they are really just residing in a potentially wet environment, and broken roots are vulnerable to the attack of fungi and bacteria, which they may not survive.

To plant or replant a delphinium root, dig out a large hole of sufficient depth to accommodate the plant. In a newly prepared bed, fork a handful of general fertilizer into the bottom of the hole, while remembering to add compost to a pre-existing site. Carefully lower your plant, and spread out the roots as far as possible. Fill the hole with loose soil, working it in and among the fibrous roots. Tread down the soil around the plant carefully to firm it in, but try not to apply excess pressure on wet or heavy soil, which will prevent the soil draining properly and cause waterlogging. If the plant has a lot of top-growth, water after planting, add 3–4 small canes for support and tie round these with twine. Shade netting can also be attached, if necessary.

Feeding and Watering the Plants

While you have added nutrients for your newly planted delphiniums that should suffice for their first year of growth, established plants also need attention during the late winter, or early spring, depending on the weather conditions. First, ensure that the area around the plants is free from weeds, then sprinkle 2–3 large handfuls (about a teacupful) of general fertilizer or blood, fish and bonemeal on the soil around the plant. Carefully fork in this fertilizer, taking care not to damage any surface roots. It is sensible to take precautions against slug and snail attack since the newly emerging shoots are a great delicacy to these pests. Unless you are growing your plants for a flower show, no further fertilizer will be required for the remainder of the year. For a show bloom or a special event, the nutrient levels can be boosted by foliar sprays of seaweed-based fertilizer or by liquid feeding of a fertilizer high in nitrogen early in the season. This can be followed later by a preparation high in potash to strengthen stems and enhance flower colour. However, do not over-feed, as the soft growth that may result is very vulnerable to weather damage.

Delphiniums require adequate supplies of water throughout their growing season, and especially during the period of spike expansion. If you look at your plants when it is raining, you can see that the crown is protected from excess water by the canopy of leaves above, so that water is directed around the plant where there are abundant fibrous roots. When you water with a hosepipe, it is too easy to soak the crown and the immediate surroundings, which can lead to rot developing in the crown. Therefore it is better to use a sprinkling attachment and to water from above until the flower spikes have started to colour, after which you may have to water directly if the weather is very dry. Many people use seep hoses, especially if they have very sandy soils. If you use this method of watering, ensure that the hose line is not directly over the crown of the plant. Parallel hose lines on either side will ensure the surroundings are moist. One way of reducing the amount of watering required is to add a thick layer of mulch after weeding and watering the ground thoroughly. A useful material to use is spent mushroom compost or leaf mould; both of these materials suppress weed growth as a bonus. You can use well-rotted manure, but this often contains seeds of weeds.

Thinning and Supporting the Stems

Many cultivars produce a large number of shoots and if these were all allowed to grow to flowering, the results would be spikes of poor quality. An established plant with adequate nutrients should support the growth of five to ten good blooms. At the base of such plants in the early spring, you may find as many as 30–40 shoots sprouting (see **Figure 6.1b**). A preliminary thinning can be done when the shoots are a few centimetres long, and can be used to provide cutting material if the shoots are taken from the base of the crown (see chapter 7). The main thinning should be done when the shoots are around 30 centimetres (12 inches) in length. At this time any shoots that are malformed – that is, flattened or distorted – can be seen and removed first. Then any other damaged shoots and those with thin, weedy stems should be removed. The number of strong stems left will depend on the vigour of the plant, from two to three for a young plant or second-year seedling to around ten on

LEFT: **Figure 6.1b.** An established delphinium plant, **'Faust'**, needs thinning.

an established plant in a herbaceous border. Use a sharp knife to cut down the stems at ground level, but do not cut into the crown. Remember to sterilize the knife blade as you move from plant to plant (see **Figure 6.1c**). After thinning, the plants look very dishevelled, but they quickly improve and the remaining stems rapidly thicken up. The stems are soft and very vulnerable to wind damage or late snowfall. Support these shoots by placing a few small canes around each plant and tie a single strand of twine from cane to cane (see **Figure 6.1d**).

The way you support mature delphinium plants, or any herbaceous perennial, is a matter of personal choice. When plants are of the small, branching type, twiggy sticks will suffice, but even the blooms of dwarf delphiniums such as 'Blue Fountains' will break off in the wind if they are heavy with rain. We cannot bear to see our blooms or plants wrecked by wind and heavy rain, so we use long bamboo canes. Three or four canes are inserted round each plant quite early in the season and the first

ABOVE: **Figure 6.1c.**
Use a sharp knife to remove surplus delphinium shoots.

RIGHT: **Figure 6.1d.**
Use canes and twine to support the stems.

tie of twine is made from cane to cane around the plant at a low level (see **Figure 6.1e**). As the plant grows, at least one further tie is added at the level of the top leaves of the plant. Some people will prefer to use canes that do not extend higher than the leaves and trust that the blooms will not be damaged. We use taller canes and add a further tie of thinner twine near the top of the spike (see **Figure 6.1f**). Blooms can now sway within the cane/twine circle without swinging far from the vertical. Remember to place caps on the tops of canes to avoid damage to your eyes. When the flowers are open for you to enjoy, these canes seem less noticeable, and the reward is far fewer breakages during bad weather. It is true that sometimes gales inevitably arrive during flowering time and damage the plants. Nor can the canes always withstand the weight of the plant, and may break, but nevertheless the likelihood of plant damage is lessened. While working among your plants check for signs of mildew, or damage by caterpillars (see chapter 9) and spray if necessary.

ABOVE: **Figure 6.1e.**
Support delphinium plants with canes and twine, and add mulch to them to lessen drying out.

LEFT: **Figure 6.1f.**
Add a 'top tie' of thin twine to retain delphinium blooms within a 'cage'.

Maintenance During the Flowering Period

Once the spike has expanded, floret development is dependent on temperature and, to some extent, the particular cultivar being grown. Some plants may develop to the extent that colour shows in many flower buds before opening, while others may slowly develop colour and open while the top of the spike is still relatively undeveloped. Generally speaking, in June the main spike in our current garden hybrids will be at its best for about three weeks, but later in early July, especially if rather hot, the spikes come out rapidly and do not last as long. For this reason we do not feel that selection of seedlings to prolong the season is very worthwhile, but there is some merit in working towards plants flowering earlier, in late May, since the flowers are longer-lasting. The display in the borders is maintained by the development of the side spikes or laterals, so care should be taken to tie in these 'branches' around the basal region of the main spike, which will by now be losing colour and developing seed pods. If you are selecting your own seedlings for use in the border, save those that have a plentiful supply of laterals.

Unless you are collecting seed, cut off the main spikes at the level of the top leaves when the blooms have faded. Likewise, the laterals should be removed a little later. At this time, the plants are producing new crown buds for the next season's growth, and it is important to maintain the water supply. Many plants fail from lack of care during the summer months when thoughts turn to holidays!

Many plants produce fresh growth from the crown due to the development of minor buds. Should you want some autumn colour from your delphiniums, they should be cut down to ground level. Again it is important to thin out these new stems, support them with new canes and, additionally, feed them with a high nitrogen fertilizer. Careful watering and observation are needed at this time of the year, since caterpillar damage is much more common and mildew may be more prevalent, especially as these shoots will probably be surrounded by other tall plants in your border.

Autumn and Winter Care

As winter approaches, the leafy flower stems wither and die down and should now be cut off about 2.5 centimetres (1 inch) above ground level. Depending on weather conditions, fresh leaves may develop late in the year, and these should be left, to avoid 'bleeding' from the crown. They will die down eventually and can be removed when they do. Remove all canes and stack on one side for cleaning later. The surrounding ground should be cleared of any weed growth and crowns can be covered by coarse sand to deter slugs and snails. Delphiniums are hardy and do not require protection from frost by material such as straw or fleece, which will harbour pests. While you are tidying up, check that all plant labels are in position and are still legible. Try pulling on stems of the dormant plants to see whether they are firmly attached to the crown. If one or two stems pull out and their bases show extensive rotting, then the plant is probably in a poor state of health and may not survive the winter. If any plants disintegrate, then dig out the remnants of the root system and add some compost to the site in preparation for next spring.

During the winter months, check the dormant delphinium plants regularly – weeding if necessary – and maintain a continuous attack on slugs and snails. If labels have been displaced by frost heave or bird activity, replace them. Finally, with the chores done for the season, look at your photographs or video and decide on replacement seedlings for next year, preparing some additional space if required.

7. Delphinium Propagation

We should not expect that delphiniums will flower well in our gardens year after year without attention simply because they are herbaceous perennials. If you do, the quantity and quality of the flowers invariably declines. Even with good cultivation practices that maintain soil fertility, delphiniums often grow less vigorously as their woody crowns become more extensive with age. The flower display can then be improved if you have a supply of vigorous young plants as replacements.

There are several ways to obtain vigorous young delphiniums from favourite mature plants. The plants can be propagated by lifting and dividing the rootstock and replanting pieces, by rooting single shoots cut from the crown, or by saving seeds and raising seedlings. Cultivated delphiniums generally do not breed true from seeds, so only the plants raised from divisions or cuttings will be identical with the starting material.

Propagation by Division

It is useful to begin by considering how the rootstock or crown of a mature delphinium plant develops. A young plant raised from seed or a cutting first grows a single flower stem, then buds for more shoots develop at the base of this stem. Later in the season, or the following year, new flowering stems develop from these basal buds. The base of each stem then becomes a source of new shoots in subsequent years. The rootstock thus develops rather like a snowflake, with a star-like group of connections radiating from each old stem, and becoming steadily broader as the plant ages.

It is clearly not sensible to divide a delphinium with this kind of root stock unless connections between sections have become sufficiently extended so that they can be severed without seriously damaging the pieces at either end. Typically this

means that division should only be used for plants that are more than four or five years old. It is much better to propagate younger plants by taking off individual shoots in spring and rooting them as cuttings.

The best time to divide mature delphiniums is in early spring, when new root growth has begun, because the divisions will then begin to establish immediately after replanting. The first step is to lift the plant out of the ground when soil conditions allow this to be done without causing excessive root damage. Carefully examine the groupings of young shoots and, if possible, locate subsurface connections between growth centres. Look for a line across the plant that appears to divide the new shoots into distinct groups, then insert a pair of garden forks back to back into the root system (see **Figure7.1a**). Lever the forks against one another to break the rootstock into two or more sections. Examine the pieces of the rootstock to check for any signs of rotting of the crown. The interconnections of the rootstock are typically hollowed-out sections of woody material, but tissue exposed at the break should be almost white and free from signs of blackening due

Figure 7.1. Preparing material for propagation.

LEFT: **Figure 7.1a.** Lever forks against each other to break rootstock.

RIGHT: **Figure 7.1b.** A clean break shows no signs of rot in the crown.

to rot (see **Figure 7.1b**). Excess woody crown material, especially any rotten material, can be trimmed away using a sharp blade to leave a plant section with shoots emerging from a solid crown and as much root as possible. Dust any cut surface on the crown with a fungicide powder before replanting the division in the ground or in a pot. Divisions should begin to grow and develop new roots in about four to five weeks, as for cuttings.

Propagation by Taking Cuttings

A disadvantage of generating new plants by dividing an old delphinium is that any diseases that affected the original plant are retained in the remaining piece of the old rootstock. This problem is reduced when plants are raised from cuttings because the new plant is forced to develop an entirely new root system.

Delphiniums are often seen as difficult to grow from cuttings, but this is not true. The secret is to start with a clear understanding of the structure of a delphinium stem and where it should be detached from the parent plant. Any inexperienced grower intending to take cuttings of a valuable delphinium should first lift an expendable plant, such as an unwanted seedling starting into growth in spring, and wash off all the soil in order to familiarize themselves with the nature of the crown and the new shoots growing out from it.

In describing the structure of a mature delphinium rootstock it was noted in chapter 1 that new-flowering stems develop from the base of old stems. The crucial point is that this ability to generate buds that will grow to new flower stems is restricted to a small region of crown tissue right at the base of the new shoot. For a cutting that will root and subsequently grow further stems, it is essential that the shoot is cut off right at the junction to the old crown, or even with a piece of old crown attached. The cutting then has this essential region of crown tissue at the base of the shoot, which is often seen as a smooth, brownish region that sometimes already has signs of new basal bud development.

Delphinium cuttings are best taken as soon as plants start into growth in early spring, and when the shoots are short and firm in texture. The task is easiest if plants are lifted from the ground, and commercial growers often lift plants in mid-winter so as to start them into early growth on a glasshouse bench. Cuttings can be taken from plants in the ground by first scraping soil away from the root so that the point of attachment of the shoot to the crown can be clearly seen. Delphiniums growing in pots can be especially difficult to work with, as tightly wound roots often impede access to the base of the shoots.

The crown of a delphinium can be hard, so a sharp steel knife or scalpel is required to detach shoots. The use of a knife always carries the risk that virus diseases may be transmitted from one plant to another. It is therefore desirable to sterilize the cutting blade before working on a plant, or keep it in a pot of sterilant solution, as is common practice for sweet-pea growers using scissors to remove tendrils from plants. It is occasionally possible to detach shoots by snapping them off at the base rather than by using a blade, but this is a very unreliable procedure that normally destroys the shoot.

Shoots for cuttings can be of any size, from basal buds with leaves just beginning to grow out of the top to shoots up to 45 centimetres (18 inches) long. In general

it is preferable to select shoots 5–15 centimetres (2–6 inches) long with a stem about 1 centimetre (⅜ inch) or less in thickness. Thicker shoots are frequently soft and are more prone to rotting during the rooting period. The highest shoots on an old stem also seldom make good cuttings, since they are the most likely to have signs of rot in their base.

When detaching a shoot for a cutting, make the cut right at the junction of the shoot with the crown (see **Figures 7.1c and 7.1d**), or make the cut into the crown and trim off the old crown tissue later. There is often a constriction in the diameter of the shoot at the junction.

Cleaning and trimming the base of delphinium cuttings before placing them in

TOP LEFT: **Figure 7.1c.** Make a cut at the junction of the shoot and the crown to obtain a cutting.

TOP RIGHT: **Figure 7.1d.** Shoots carefully detached from the crown.

BOTTOM LEFT: **Figure 7.1e.** Wash off any soil particles under a running tap.

BOTTOM RIGHT: **Figure 7.1f.** Pare off tissue to leave a clean base to a shoot.

a rooting medium is desirable because such basal shoots have been in the ground and are likely to be contaminated with soil and disease organisms. First wash dirt from the lower section of the shoot under a running tap and then pick off any decaying remnants of leaf scales (see **Figure 7.1e**). A brush can be used to dislodge dirt, but be careful not to damage any tiny buds on the basal region. Use a sharp knife blade or scalpel to trim off any old crown tissue. The base of the shoot should then be solid with no hole into the hollow stem of the shoot, and free from any obvious black staining due to rot. Dark staining is not *always* caused by rot, since it could also result from oxidation of stem tissue freshly exposed to the air after cutting. If there is a small amount of dark staining, it is worth paring off thin slices from the base of the shoot to see if a clean base can be obtained (see **Figure 7.1f**). The limit to how much material can be removed is set by the need to retain a region of basal tissue and to avoid breaking through into the hollow part of the stem. When trimming the cuttings, strip off damaged leaves and their stalks. For long shoots it is advantageous to retain just two leaves and the tuft of unexpanded leaves at the top.

In preparing delphinium cuttings ourselves, we normally stand the cuttings in a sterilant solution after cleaning and trimming them. For this purpose we use a dilute solution of a sterilant for babies' feeding bottles that contains sodium hypochlorite as the active agent. The prepared cuttings are stood in the solution with the lower 3–5 centimetres (1–2 inches) of stem immersed for 3–5 minutes and then rinsed under a running tap.

Rooting Prepared Cuttings

There are many alternative rooting media for prepared delphinium cuttings. Some gardeners simply push cuttings into holes in the soil and then firm the soil around them. Some commercial growers insert cuttings in trays of moist sand. After routinely experiencing high losses when attempting to root cuttings in soil or compost mixes, we adopted two methods originally advocated in articles in past issues of the Delphinium Society's *Year Book*. The first is the simple procedure of rooting the cuttings in a jar of water, and the second is to use horticultural Perlite, an expanded volcanic rock material, as a sterile rooting medium. After adopting these methods, and the cleaning and sterilization procedures described above, losses during the rooting period dropped to a tolerably low level.

Rooting in Perlite produces cuttings with superb root systems, and is our preferred procedure. Rooting in jars of water is not quite as effective but is easily used when only one or two cuttings of a cultivar are available, and is the best method for long shoots taken as cuttings from plants that have grown beyond the ideal stage.

For rooting cuttings in water, we keep a collection of clean glass jars in a range of sizes. For shoots 15 centimetres (6 inches) long, for example, a jar about 10 centimetres (4 inches) tall is selected and sufficient clean tap water is added to give a water depth of approximately 4 cm (1½ inches) in the bottom. Depending on the diameter of the jar, up to five or six prepared cuttings of a single cultivar are then stood in the jar with their bases immersed in the water. The jar is then clearly labelled so that the cultivar is identifiable. Before placing the cuttings in water, we normally dust their basal region with a hormone rooting powder containing a fungicide. The water level in jars should be checked daily and replenished as necessary (see **Figure 7.2a**).

Figure 7.2. Rooting delphinium cuttings.

RIGHT: **Figure 7.2a.** Prepared cuttings ready to root in a jar of water.

When horticultural Perlite is used as the rooting medium, dwarf pots 10–15 centimetres (4–6 inches) in diameter are filled with Perlite, which is then thoroughly soaked with clean water. The cutting is then inserted into a hole made in the rooting medium about 2.5–4 centimetres (1–1½ inches) deep, which is then filled in by moving the surrounding Perlite to hold the shoot in place. Insert long cuttings more deeply to ensure that they are adequately supported. Pour water from a can with a fine spout down the stem of the cutting to ensure that it is firmly supported and that the base is in capillary contact with the rooting medium. Up to eight evenly spaced cuttings can be rooted in a pot with a diameter of 15 centimetres (6 inches). Add a label to identify the cultivar and stand the pot in a saucer of clean water. The water level should be checked daily and topped up as necessary (see **Figure 7.2b**).

Cuttings in Perlite normally need no other support than that provided by the rooting medium. If it is necessary to root long shoots, these can be supported by tying them with twine to split canes up to 40 centimetres (16 inches) long inserted in the Perlite. The support canes should be tied together at the top to form a tripod that is sufficiently stable to support a plastic bag placed over the pot of cuttings, which helps to avoid wilting in the early stages of the rooting process.

Light is important for rooting, so cuttings being rooted in jars of water or pots of Perlite should be placed in good light, for example on the bench in a cool glasshouse or on a window ledge indoors, but shaded from strong sunlight. We do not find it necessary to use additional bottom heat to accelerate rooting of delphinium cuttings, although other growers tell us that rooting times are significantly reduced if trays of cuttings are placed on a slightly heated bench. We do not recommend that large numbers of cuttings be supported by mesh in a single tray of water, or that several pots of cuttings in Perlite share a common water tray, since such methods could result in disease transmission between batches of cuttings.

The rooting time for delphinium cuttings is long compared with that for, say, chrysanthemums. It decreases significantly as day length and temperature increase during spring, from about 5 weeks during February/March to 4 weeks or less in April. We have found that rooting cuttings later in the season than this becomes more difficult and is associated with a greatly increased failure rate.

ABOVE LEFT: **Figure 7.2b.** Cuttings inserted in moist Perlite and standing in a saucer of water.

ABOVE RIGHT: **Figure 7.2c.** Stems 'growing out' indicate that rooting has commenced.

The progress of rooting for cuttings in a jar of water is easily monitored because the basal region of the shoot can be seen without removing it from the rooting medium. Cuttings in Perlite can be easily removed for inspection and watered in again after replacement. However, the appearance of the upper part of the shoot is usually a sufficient guide. Cuttings normally go downhill for two to three weeks, with some leaves yellowing and withering. Decaying material should be removed to avoid problems with *botrytis* (grey mould). If a cutting fails to take up water and wilts, it should be removed and a slice of tissue cut from the base in an effort to reopen blocked capillaries in the base. After the initial period of decline, leaves in the growth point look fresher and the stem begins to grow out, indicating that root formation has begun (see **Figure 7.2c**). However, the stem can extend by 5 centimetres (2 inches) or more without there being sufficient root to justify removing the cutting for potting up. The progress of root development for cuttings in Perlite can be assessed by gently tugging on the stem, as a well-rooted shoot becomes very firmly anchored in the pot. A well-rooted cutting has many new roots emerging in a ring all round the base (see **Figure 7.2d**).

Cuttings should be removed from the rooting medium and potted up in a pot of 9–10 centimetres (3½–4 inches) diameter filled with moist multipurpose potting compost as soon as the roots are about 1–4 centimetres (½–1½ inches) long. It is advantageous to pot up cuttings from water with short roots, as root development on these is likely to be inferior to those that have been rooted in Perlite. When potting up a batch of cuttings in Perlite, any shoots with insufficient root should be replaced in the rooting medium, watered in and left to grow for a few more days. Shoots showing any sign of rot in the base should be discarded straight away.

It is useful to place a short split cane alongside the cutting when potting up. This eliminates the risk of damaging the stem or roots by inserting a support cane when the pot is full of compost. In warm spring weather, new roots grow quickly and should be found emerging from the base of the pot within a few days. At this stage, or when potting up the cuttings, pinch out the tip of the growing point of the shoot in order to stimulate development of new shoots from the base of the cutting (see **Figure 7.2e**). New stems should emerge from the compost alongside the original stem after four to five weeks (see **Figure

ABOVE: **Figure 7.2f.** New shoots break from the base of this cutting.

7.2f). Once a cutting has developed these 'breaks' it is a fully functional plant that can be planted out in the garden or distributed to other growers. Despite looking healthy and having a good root system, cuttings are sometimes slow to break from the base, or fail to do so in the first season. This problem seems more common for cuttings taken late in spring, but is probably also cultivar-dependent. So long as the basal region of the shoot has not been damaged by rot, for example, the plant may develop normally in the following season.

Micropropagation

Although for the average gardener, taking cuttings will be adequate to maintain named delphinium cultivars for the border, for those wanting large numbers of a favourite plant or for commercial suppliers it is a relatively slow method of propagation.

Two factors influence the yield of new plants; the number of shoots produced by the cultivar and the need to use basal shoots either early in the year or shortly after flowering. Ideally, material should be available throughout the gardening year.

Micropropagation, which is propagation from very small amounts of material, offers a means of increasing the number of daughter plants that can be grown from each individual parent plant.

Unlike most animal cells, all plant cells are capable of dedifferentiation, that is, changing from a specific form such as leaf tissue back to an unprogrammed state. Then, with the appropriate stimuli, they can differentiate to produce a new plant. Thus under the right conditions, roots, shoots or leaves can be made to produce new plants. Material from the shoot tip, the meristem, can also be used, but right at the tip it is actually undifferentiated. However, it takes time to set the clock back and restart cellular processes. Producing plants from basal cuttings is rather similar: the programme has to be changed. The dedifferentiated tissue from roots, shoots or leaves is termed callus, and if you look at the cut end of a cutting after 2 to 3 weeks, you can see callus appearing, from which new roots will emerge.

While we sterilize the cut end of the basal shoot during the preparation of our cuttings, the production of callus and new roots occurs in a non-sterile environment, and sometimes the shoots will go rotten. During micropropagation, a sterile environment is essential since bacteria and moulds will quickly overgrow the tiny piece of tissue.

The material to be used, for example from a leaf, is sterilized, and using a binocular microscope it is dissected with a sterile knife blade into tiny pieces called 'explants'. This step has to be done in an environment as clean and dust-free as possible – for commercial production it is done in a laminar flow cabinet. Explants are transferred to petri dishes or test tubes containing sterile growth medium, usually combined with agar as a support medium. The growth medium that is generally available as a basic mix contains mineral salts, sucrose and vitamins to mimic the cellular environment. To this is added the appropriate ratio of hormones – either auxins to stimulate root growth or cytokinins for shoots. The exact balance of

Figure 7.3.
Micropropagation of
delphiniums.

RIGHT: **Figure 7.3a.** An
explant of young delphinium
leaf tissue on agar has
become a callus.

RIGHT: **Figure 7.3b.**
Formation of leaves from
delphinium callus after
stimulation by high levels
of cytokinin.

RIGHT: **Figure 7.3c.**
Formation of roots from
delphinium callus after
stimulation by high levels
of auxin.

ingredients in the basic mix has to be determined for each plant family or species, or even cultivar. The tiny explant set up on agar has to be kept at a constant temperature, which is dependent on the plant species, but usually around 18–20°C (64–68°F), and under constant light provided by fluorescent daylight lamps for a fixed day-length, usually of 16 hours. When viewed under a microscope, the appearance of the explant changes with time from an organized and recognizable fragment of leaf tissue to callus, a jumble of dedifferentiated cells (see **Figure 7.3a**). Moving the explant under sterile conditions onto hormone regimes, a high cytokinin/auxin ratio will produce shoot cells, while high auxin/cytokinin will produce root cells. The auxin often used is familiar, indole acetic acid (IAA), which is present in the hormone rooting powder that is used when taking cuttings. By manipulation of these levels of hormone, the callus is stimulated to produce differentiated material, at first a large number of shoots (see **Figures 7.3b and 7.3c**). If these are carefully separated under sterile conditions and placed on agar with high auxin, a large number of plantlets can be obtained.

These young plantlets are used to a very protected environment, with high humidity and no air movement. The next difficult step is to 'wean' the plantlets off this environment by exposure to conditions that progressively approximate those of the outside world. Plantlets can be placed in small peat 'jiffy' pots in trays covered by a plastic cover. Over a period of several weeks, the amount of ventilation is increased gradually so that the growing plant can tolerate fresh air. The whole procedure – from taking the explant to obtaining plants growing outside the laboratory – may take three months, and explants can continue producing new plantlets, providing sterility is strictly maintained.

There are problems associated with micropropagation, namely ensuring that the final plantlets are genetically identical to the original cultivar. If the material used is other than the meristem (the extremely small amount of undifferentiated material at the tip of the shoot), plantlets may show small genetic changes. Additionally, for many plants the procedures have not been developed. The Ranunculaceae have been a difficult family to micropropagate, in part due to browning of the medium and explant. This will not be surprising to gardeners who handle delphiniums. There are now laboratories that produce micropropagated delphinium cultivars in enormous numbers, but the technique is probably not one to be tackled by other than the very keen amateur or semi-professional grower.

Propagation from Seed

Taking cuttings and division both allow you to maintain named delphiniums or seedlings received from friends, but a larger number of plants differing in colour or height can be readily obtained by growing them from seed. This could be open-pollinated seed, or you may have purchased some of the excellent-quality F1 hybrid seed available, or perhaps experimented with hybridization to produce your own hand-pollinated seed. Whatever your source of seed, it needs to be offered the best conditions to germinate. Rather than broadcast them in the open ground where there are no means of regulating conditions, sow them in containers of sterilized seed compost.

Sowing your Seeds
Delphinium seed can be sown at any time of year, but either late winter to early spring or early autumn are most suitable. Starting early and treating the seeds as if delphiniums were half-hardy annuals allows you to see one flower spike per plant within 6 months of sowing. This is ideal if you want to know the results of hand-pollination, as we do, so we sow our seeds in mid-to-late February. For those of a less impatient nature, any time until late March or early April will give strong plants that may flower the same year. It is not advisable to sow during the summer months when

temperatures remain high, but seeds can be sown in September when the weather is cooler. This provides you with seedlings large enough to over-winter in pots.

Garden hybrid delphinium seed requires a temperature range from 15–20°C (59–68°F) for successful germination. Excessive heat is a common cause of germination failures. Low temperatures are not harmful but slow down germination, so that there is an increased risk of the seeds rotting due to the presence of moulds in the compost or on the seed coat. Under good conditions, garden delphiniums will germinate 10 to 28 days after sowing but may take longer. This often depends on the age or the parentage of the seed. Seed from dark blue or dusky-pink cultivars will often germinate sporadically over a long time, while other seed may show at least two peaks of germination.

As delphinium seed germinates relatively slowly and the seed must be kept moist throughout this period, use commercial peat-based multipurpose compost as the sowing medium. This compost needs to be sterile, so buy a good-quality brand and do not reuse compost unless you have some means of sterilizing it. We add horticultural vermiculite to compost to improve texture, and also the root growth of the seedlings. You can add coarse sand to achieve a similar result, but be certain that the sand has been sufficiently washed to remove salts. While loam-based composts may retain moisture better, they will favour the damping-off fungus Pythium, and you will soon lose your seedlings in an attack.

Seeds should be sown thinly on the surface of moist compost in either a clean plastic pot or seed tray. Label the container clearly with the cross or variety of seed. We sow 40 seeds in 9-centimetre (3½-inch) pots (**Figure 7.4a**). Alternatively, you can use plug trays, placing seeds in individual cells. Cover the seeds with a thin layer of compost and place the container in a saucer or larger tray of water for a few minutes to ensure that the compost is thoroughly moist. Remove from the water, allow any excess moisture to drain away, and then cover with a piece of kitchen foil (see

Figure 7.4. Germinating delphinium seed.

RIGHT: **Figure 7.4a.** Sow delphinium seeds thinly.

FAR RIGHT: **Figure 7.4b.** Cover pot with kitchen foil to prevent moisture loss.

RIGHT: **Figure 7.4c.** Seedlings emerging 10 days after sowing.

FAR RIGHT: **Figure 7.4d.** Seedlings under a transparent cover.

Figure 7.4b). Place the containers where you can maintain the temperature at 15–20°C (59–68°F); we use the bathroom, but as long as the temperature is maintained at a relatively constant level, any spot will be adequate. Do not use a heated propagator at a high setting.

After about seven days it is advisable to carefully remove the foil cap daily and look for signs of germination. As soon as five or more seedlings have emerged, remove the foil cover and move the container into good light to avoid etiolation (see **Figure 7.4c**). Do not place the container in direct sunlight, which will scorch and destroy young seedlings very rapidly. To ensure that the remaining seeds germinate, the surface of the compost must remain moist, so cover the container with a transparent cover to reduce evaporation. However, this action will also favour conditions for damping-off, so increase the ventilation by raising the cover a little as soon as a good proportion of the seedlings have emerged (see **Figure 7.4d**). Do not worry if the seed coat fails to fall off the cotyledons (seed leaves) completely; however, this does prevent 'greening', and thus the ability of the seed leaves to photosynthesize. If you are brave enough and conditions are moist, very gently remove the old seed coat using a pair of tweezers.

An alternative method of germinating seeds is that of 'chitting' the seed, rather like growing mustard and cress or sweet peas. A piece of wet, plain paper kitchen towel is spread over the base of a small box that can be closed with a lid. The seeds are distributed evenly over the moist base and covered with another piece of wet kitchen towel (see **Figure 7.4e**). The box is closed

ABOVE: **Figure 7.4e.** Root emergence in seeds 'chitted' on wet paper kitchen towel.

ABOVE: **Figure 7.4f.** Planting an individual seed with an emerging root.

and placed in an environment with the temperature at 15–20°C (59–68°F). As soon as the seeds show an emerging root, each can be carefully removed using tweezers and placed individually just below the surface of moist compost in a 5-centimetre (2-inch) pot or in a cell of a plug tray (see **Figure 7.4f**). These pots must be kept under a transparent cover until the cotyledons emerge in 2–3 days. Although time-consuming, this method has two advantages. The germination rate will be known precisely, and in a cross where the germination period is prolonged, every viable seed will be obtained. Furthermore, the need for 'pricking-out' – and thus root disturbance – is avoided, with the contents of the smaller pot being transferred directly to a larger one when roots have developed sufficiently.

Pricking out Seedlings

Depending on conditions, for example the amount of available light, the first true leaf grows from the junction of the cotyledons in about three weeks. Do not prick out seedlings before the true leaves appear, or you will probably lose them. It is advisable to wait a little longer until a second true leaf appears, but not too long because although the visible seedling is relatively small, root growth will already be extensive (see **Figure 7.5a**). With care, prick out seedlings into individual 9-centimetre (3½-inch) pots filled with good quality, moist multipurpose compost, and make sure to label the pots (see **Figure 7.5b**). Allow seedlings to stabilize and stand the pots in good light and a cool place. After about 1–2 weeks, when they are obviously growing, harden them off and place outside, where they will grow rapidly. If possible, offer some protection from heavy rain or late frost (see **Figure 7.5c**).

Around mid-May to mid-June (from a mid-February to mid-March sowing), seedlings will have three or more well-grown adult leaves, and their roots will be filling the pot (see **Figure 7.5d**). Try to avoid seedlings becoming pot-bound by planting them out as soon as weather conditions allow.

If you do not obtain delphinium seed in time to start growing in March, or if you will be away from home during the time that the seedlings need attention, delay sowing seeds until September. We have known growers living in much hotter climates who, after sowing, surround the seed pans with iced water in order to obtain lower temperatures for germination. If you sow later in the year, seedlings will not be large enough to plant in the open ground and should be left in pots to over-winter, preferably with overhead protection from heavy rain. The seedlings will die down and become dormant before re-growth in the spring, when they can be planted out.

Figure 7.5. Growing delphinium seedlings.

RIGHT: **Figure 7.5a.** Seedlings with one or two true leaves ready for pricking out.

FAR RIGHT: **Figure 7.5b.** Seedlings pricked out into 9-centimetre (3½-inch) pots of moist compost.

RIGHT: **Figure 7.5c.** Give seedlings some protection from heavy rain or late frosts.

FAR RIGHT: **Figure 7.5d.** Well-grown seedlings ready for planting out.

Growing Seedlings

When growing seedlings, you will not know about the quality, or perhaps even the colour, of the flower. Seedlings start as very small plants, so it is not sensible to place them in a border where other plants will shade them and compete for water. You need to select an area of ground to grow your seedlings – for example, a vegetable patch or a bed cleared of other plants, or perhaps even sacrifice an area of lawn. Wherever you choose, first prepare the ground a few weeks before you intend to plant out by digging in compost and a generous quantity of compound fertilizer. When the soil is moist but not wet, plant out the seedlings in rows with gaps of at least 30 centimetres (12 inches) between plants. You can have two rows separated by 30 centimetres and then a gap of 60 centimetres (24 inches) between these rows and the next pair (see **Figure 7.5e**). Yes, delphiniums are large perennials, but at this point you are only looking to see one spike per plant for assessment, not placing them in a permanent growing position.

In order to give each seedling a good start, fork a teaspoonful of dried blood (or high-nitrogen fertilizer) into the bottom of the planting hole. Plant the seedling and place a handful of coarse sand around the neck of the young plant in an attempt to deter slugs and snails. If the weather becomes very dry, keep the soil moist by watering, and add a mulch of mushroom compost or leaf mould to conserve moisture and reduce weed growth. Should the weather become really hot and sunny just after you have planted out your seedlings, erect some shade netting to aid establishment.

If you have too many seedlings to plant out and wish to keep those that remain, continue to re-pot them into progressively larger pots or containers. Although it is possible to obtain flower spikes from plants in 1-litre pots, they are really only useful for an assessment of colour and it is much better to use 2-litre or larger pots. Alternatively, take your plants to a local plant sale, or encourage your neighbours to grow some good plants.

ABOVE: **Figure 7.5e.** Rows of newly planted seedlings.

Seedlings planted out in the open ground from an early sowing will make rapid growth during late June and July, providing there is sufficient moisture. Leaves will enlarge dramatically and after about five months (18–20 weeks) will produce a sturdy flower stem that thickens as it grows. We do not favour the procedure of pinching out this shoot unless it is damaged. The stems require support, as they are vulnerable to breakage at the young crown in strong winds and rain, resulting in loss of the plant. Individual staking is unrealistic, so place canes (at least 1.2 metres/47 inches in height) along each row at every third or fourth plant and then weave twine between these canes at an appropriate height to the growing plants (see **Figure 7.5f**). Remember to protect the tops of canes with caps. Further twine can be added at a higher level when necessary. This does not stop you putting in a taller cane to support an individual bloom that looks promising.

RIGHT: **Figure 7.5f.**
Seedlings with emerging
flower spikes.

Some growers support seedlings using a horizontal lattice of pig-wire with a mesh of 15 centimetres (6 inches) or a net with a mesh large enough to allow the young plants to grow up through it. These mesh cages can be carefully raised to support the plants as they grow.

Working with the plants allows you to check for any onset of powdery mildew and treat with the appropriate fungicide. Keep a watchful eye for the presence of caterpillars (see chapter 9), removing any that are seen.

Around six months after sowing your seed, you should have some lovely flowers to enjoy, and there will be a succession of new flowers until the onset of lower temperatures and decreasing day-length slows development. This extends the season for delphiniums from the main peak of adult plants in mid-June/early July into August, September and early October. In favourable years, we often have a few blooms in November. All these seedlings will go dormant and require care over the winter months. However, they will be far too close together to grow adequately in the following season, and a delphinium jungle would quickly arise. This means that while enjoying the seedling blooms you need to spend some time looking at the individual plants in order to select those worth retaining.

Selecting Seedlings to Retain

Since few of us can remember the features of all the seedlings grown, it is worth making notes or photographing the flowers at intervals during their flowering season. Label the seedlings at this time, as they are indistinguishable from each other once the flowers have gone.

Although seedlings flowering for the first time may not give a reliable indication of their final height, there are a number of features that you should look at while making your choice. Clearly all seedlings with defects such as single or nearly single florets, streaky colour or twisted foliage

Figure 7.6. Assessing the quality of new delphinium seedling flowers.

LEFT: **Figure 7.6a.** A white seedling with regularly arranged flat florets.

RIGHT: **Figure 7.6b.** Pink 'sister' seedlings with nicely formed florets but some irregularities in spike packing.

should be dug up and disposed of. Look for healthy green foliage, remembering that cream seedlings will, in general, have bronzy foliage. Look for flower spikes with a large number of florets regularly spaced around the stem (see **Figures 7.6a and 7.6b**). Irregular spikes are quite common, but unless there are gross irregularities, take other factors into consideration. The flowers should be organized such that the florets just touch each other in their spiral; they should neither form a 'birdcage' where the gap between florets is large, nor should florets be tightly packed. This is not an easy judgement when conditions have been particularly dry, since the spike may not have expanded properly.

In all probability, the colour of the flower will be the characteristic that most gardeners will look at in order to make their selection for future use. Remember that the time of year will influence colour development, but look for bright rather than flat, dull colours, and also for a good texture to the sepals. Whether you want florets in a pure single colour, or with blue

back sepals and purple forward sepals, for example, is a personal choice. Ensure that the floret is of good, rounded form with evenly distributed sepals, and that it opens flat rather than staying cupped (see **Figure 7.6c**). The petals should be neat and well-developed, forming a compact eye. Many growers will prefer that the eye is one colour rather than being striped with the sepal colour (see **Figure 7.6d**). If you find a double flower without any eye and more than 13 sepals – preferably 18 or more – these can be quite attractive, especially if they are bicolours, which seem to appeal to flower-arrangers. It is worth remembering that the double form may not occur when the plant flowers in June the following year.

Unless you are growing seedlings from specific hand-crosses, cream flowers will be infrequent. When they do occur in a general mixture, the plants are often weak, growing rather poorly and with foliage that leaves a lot to be desired. Such plants will often die during the first winter. However, good plants – worthy to be named cultivars – have been found among batches of seedlings, so among your seedlings there may be one that should be retained. Make allowances for growth habit in this first season and concentrate on the flower, looking for good texture, and depth of colour. If you are unsure whether you really have a cream, place a floret next to one taken from a white plant. Generally it is the eye that enhances these cream flowers, with a deep yellow being the choice of many growers. Ginger or brown eyes are also very attractive.

When decisions have been made, do *not* rush to move your selected plants. Clean up the area and make sure that it is kept free from weeds over the winter months. Place coarse sand over all the crowns and make sure all plants are labelled adequately. Since birds or other animals may disturb the plot, a plan of the bed is useful to ensure that you retain the selected plants in the spring. We strongly advise that you move your seedlings, as with mature plants, in the spring when there are obvious signs of life in the crown and the roots will start into fresh growth. Do not be too disappointed if plants that you have particularly admired fail to reappear in the spring; this happens to all of us! For this reason, the retention of all but the poorest plants offers you the chance of lower-rated plants filling in gaps in borders or plots and – you never know – they might be much better than expected. Once you have finished planting out your selected seedlings in the spring, clear the area of unwanted plants and either give them away or dispose of them so that you can utilize the ground.

ABOVE LEFT: **Figure 7.6c.** A purple floret with rounded form, evenly distributed sepals and a compact brown eye.

ABOVE RIGHT: **Figure 7.6d.** A lovely floret with an interesting colour combination.

8. Growing Delphiniums in Containers

Many gardening enthusiasts feel that their garden is too small, or their soil too heavy or sandy, to grow delphiniums successfully. In addition, many modern gardens have large areas of concrete or patio that are seen as a disincentive to growing perennials. However, these difficulties may be overcome by growing plants in containers, allowing colourful displays of flowers throughout the year (see **Figure 8.1a**).

Delphiniums of all types, from garden hybrids with large blooms to dwarf species, can be very successful in suitable containers, which offer many advantages in that they are mobile. They can be grown in one area and moved to another to give a display when just coming into flower, then moved again when the flowers have finished. If seed is required, they do not have to be cut down immediately and can be allowed to ripen the seed without becoming unsightly in a border. The flowering period can be brought forward or delayed by the choice of a suitable site, so that a longer display can be obtained. Plants required for use as parents in delphinium breeding can also be readily brought under cover when crosses are being made. Containers also make an ideal way of growing species delphiniums, since they can be afforded suitable planting media, greater care in positioning and, under protection, the period of dormancy that they require after flowering.

Figure 8.1. Delphiniums in containers.

RIGHT: **Figure 8.1a.** Pot-grown delphiniums along a path make a colourful feature.

Potting up the Plants

When growing delphiniums in containers, it is important to start with a young plant in good condition. The plants should be either young, vigorous seedlings or newly rooted cuttings. Young plants will need to be potted on progressively into larger pots until of a sufficient size to be placed in their final container. It is unwise to put a very small plant into a large pot, since it will be surrounded by an excess of wet compost. Selected seedlings should be dug up from the open ground in spring before vigorous new root growth makes the soil ball too large and heavy. Circumstances do not always allow for spring planting and you may, for example, have to move house. If you wish to save a particular plant at such a time, you may be successful in transferring it to a container, providing care is taken to minimize root damage.

We prefer 7.5-litre (25-centimetre/ 10-inch) plastic pots as the final size of container for *elatum* cultivars, as these are relatively easy to move (see **Figure 8.1b**). Larger pots or tubs can be used, but they become increasingly heavy as the delphinium grows and flowers. Clay pots (terracotta) can be used of course, but they tend to become so heavy that there is a risk of back injuries when lifting the plants. It is more difficult to provide adequate water for delphiniums growing in clay pots (which dry out rather quickly during hot weather) than those in plastic pots. We have used containers of all types, including 'gro-bags' on a terrace, in which one plant will survive successfully, although it is not easy to support.

Peat-based composts help to reduce the weight of the container, and it is easier to maintain adequate levels of water using this growth medium. Many growers prefer soil-based composts because they are not subject either to the difficulty encountered in re-wetting peat-based composts that have really dried out, or the acidity that may develop in peat.

When peat-based composts are no longer available, trials of the alternatives will be needed in order to select the most suitable medium for delphiniums. When potting on cuttings or seedlings, and for growing species delphiniums, it is an advantage to add Perlite to the medium to improve the drainage. Good drainage is vital to all plants in containers, but especially for species that require adequate moisture during their short growing period, followed by dry, well-drained conditions during dormancy.

Feeding and Watering

Container-grown plants require feeding, and a number of approaches have been found successful. The requirements of the plant change as it grows, and one method is to use liquid feeding. During the early growth period, plants can be regularly fed (once a week) with a liquid fertilizer containing a high ratio of nitrogen. When they are closer to the flowering period, the fertilizer is changed to a more balanced formula (N P K – 1 1 1).

BELOW: **Figure 8.1b.** Plants grown in 25-centimetre (10-inch) plastic pots are easy to move.

Clearly this feeding regime is ideal when plants require a lot of water, but over-watering at any time can lead to loss of roots, especially early in the year. In order to overcome this problem, a top-dressing of a granular-type fertilizer such as 'RosePlus with Emag' can be used in late winter instead of liquid feeding.

Another approach is to use slow-release granules such as 'Osmocote' that, according to the manufacturer, release balanced fertilizer into the surrounding compost over a period of 4 to 6 months. Slow-release granules are incorporated into the compost at potting time and are used to 'top-dress' established plants in pots in late winter, and again after flowering in late July/early August. While the flower spike is developing, liquid feeding can be used to boost nutrient levels.

It is clear that to be successful when growing any plant in a container, attention to watering is essential. Using a watering can is preferable to a garden hose in order to reduce disturbance to the compost surface and to avoid inadvertent flooding of the pot. The crown of a delphinium in the ground is protected by its leaf canopy but, in a container, water is applied to the compost in the top of the pot and not the leaves, so one must be careful not to over-saturate the plant.

As large delphiniums approach flowering, they may need to be watered more than once a day during dry weather. Garden hybrid delphiniums in pots need to be kept well watered even after the flowers have finished blooming, since the new crown buds for next year's display are developing, and it is easy to forget your pots when going off for a summer holiday.

Thinning and Supporting the Plants

Since the root system of a container plant is restricted, delphiniums should be thinned in the spring to reduce the number of flowering stems and thus improve the quality of those remaining. During the early growth period, cut out obviously weak stems and reduce the total number to four. Growers requiring blooms for a show or special demonstration can reduce this number to two or even one at a much later stage in growth. If you do this too early, it is always possible that an attack by caterpillars will demolish your flower spike(s), leaving you without any blooms! If secondary growth at the base of the plant gives rise to a number of small stems after thinning, be ruthless and remove them (see **Figure 8.1c**).

Plants in containers are very vulnerable to wind damage during early growth, so put two bamboo canes in the compost before new roots have become extensive. Even though it looks rather foolish, use 1.2-metre (47-inch) canes and tie a ring of twine from cane to cane that encircles and supports the new growth. Put protective caps on the tops of canes, because it is too easy to be careless when bending over pots. As the stems extend, add more circles of twine until you reach the top of the cane, and probably at the top of the leaves.

BELOW: **Figure 8.1c.** Grow just two stems to obtain high-quality blooms.

In order to keep a large number of pots upright in an open site, we use a support system resembling that used by a sweet pea or chrysanthemum grower. A series of posts is driven at intervals through ground-cover fabric, such as 'Mypex', and connected by lengths of wire arranged to give a lower rail at about 60 centimetres (24 inches) and an upper one at 1.2 metres (47 inches; see **Figure 8.1d**). At appropriate intervals according to pot size, 1.8-metre (71-inch) canes are secured to the wires in an upright position using V-clips – stainless steel clips that are easy to use. String ties will do just as well, but it is a very tedious job when a large number of canes are needed. Pots are placed on the ground-cover material and tied to these upright canes via the smaller pot canes (see **Figure 8.1e**). You can tie the fully expanded flower spike loosely to the upright cane to avoid wind damage.

ABOVE: **Figure 8.1d.**
Containers placed in an open site need a support system.

LEFT: **Figure 8.1e.**
Give some extra support to plants in containers.

Care after Flowering

After flowering and, if desired, seed collection, the spikes are cut down to the level of the leaves and the plants maintained over the summer months. The old stems and any new growth from the crown should be removed during the autumn. Clean up the top surface of pots by removing weeds, liverworts and mosses. A handful of sharp sand over the crown will help to deter slugs and snails over the winter months.

A problem with all container-grown plants over the winter months, whether they be on porous ground-cover material or on a concrete patio, is waterlogging. This can be avoided by raising the pots off ground level. Since we have so many plants in pots, we use a cheap and readily obtainable material to overcome this

problem, namely 'tiling battens' sold for roofing. These battens have a very long lifetime and are sold in lengths of around 5 metres (16 feet), which you can cut to size (not least to fit them in your car!). Arranged in pairs they are an inexpensive way of raising pots off the ground (see **Figure 8.1f**). In the UK, where winters are less severe, delphiniums in containers survive periods of freezing – and indeed, a cold period is required to promote dormancy, which seems to be an essential part of the plant's lifecycle. If heavy rain follows a period of freezing temperatures it is advisable to tip off water lying on the tops of 'solid' pots.

Action must be taken against slugs and snails throughout the year by the correct use of proprietary agents. A problem with containers is that ants and woodlice can invade the compost through the basal holes. Ants in particular tunnel through compost, destroying root systems and eventually the plant, so you must check your pots regularly, looking for tell-tale heaps of compost adjacent to the basal holes. If you have a problem with ants, treat the base of the pot with an insecticide powder sold for the purpose and, if need be, re-pot your plant. Other unwelcome pests include squirrels (or in North America, chipmunks) who will under-plant your pots with a variety of nuts. Foxes also dig out pots, and this behaviour seems to be linked to the presence of rotting stems; maybe they are attracted by the smell of fungal decay – but we doubt that any truffles are present!

ABOVE: **Figure 8.1f.** Raise containers off the ground using lengths of tiling batten.

9. Pests and Diseases

Generally speaking, delphiniums do not suffer unduly from pests or diseases, many of which they share with most of our garden perennials or our food crops. However, it must be admitted that it is disheartening even to the most seasoned grower to look at plants, and particularly flowers, spoilt by pest attack or symptoms of disease. Horticultural pests are considered to be organisms that damage or destroy plants, but it should always be remembered that 'pests' may have a dual function – for example, birds may damage flowers but feed on aphids – so the treatment of any such problem needs a balanced approach.

Slugs and Snails

Probably the most common reason people give for regarding delphiniums as 'ungrowable in my garden' is the presence of slugs and snails – yet they then go on to say they grow hostas, lettuce and strawberries. These molluscs with prodigious appetites, leaving behind a slime trail as they move along on a muscular foot, actually play an important role in disposing of decaying plant materials.

The common species of slugs are the field slug, *Deroceras reticulatum*, the garden slug, *Arion hortensis*, and the keeled or subterranean slug, *Milax sp.* Field slugs are probably the most common pests of fields and gardens and are distributed worldwide. Variable in colour from light grey-brown to fawn, cream or yellowish-white, their adult size ranges between 3–5 centimetres (1¼–2 inches) in length. Also very common, the garden slug, which feeds both above and below ground, has a dark-brown, grey or black upper surface and is yellowish-orange underneath. This smaller slug, 2–3 centimetres (¾–1¼ inches) long as an adult, is less active at lower temperatures compared to the field slug,

which will feed at temperatures as low as 1°C (34°F). Both species will produce around 300 or more eggs a year. Keeled slugs feed predominantly below ground and will attack fleshy roots (potatoes are a delight!). They are black or brown with an orange or yellow keel along the centre of the back. As adults they reach 6–7 centimetres (2¼–2¾ inches), but thankfully their egg production is considerably lower than the other two species, at 30 eggs a year. Most people will recognize the monster black slug, *Arion ater*, which is 10–13 centimetres (4–5 inches) long, dark brown or black in colour, and will demolish seedlings. This species is actually less damaging to mature plants.

Among species of snails, the garden snail, *Helix aspersa*, is very common with a grey shell marked by flecks or streaks. This shell can be up to 3.8 centimetres (1½ inches) in diameter. A smaller snail, *Trichia striolata*, is also common but is less obvious. *Trichia* possesses a flattened shell, 1–3 centimetres (⅜–1¼ inches) in diameter, which is grey to red-brown in colour. More obvious, and quite common in rock gardens and near walls, are the banded snails, *Cepaea hortensis*, with a shell diameter up to 2 centimetres (¾ inch), and the slightly larger *Cepaea nemoralis*. These possess shells that are variable in colour from yellow through light brown to reddish, and are marked with up to five bands of dark colour.

Slugs and snails damage leaves – leaving irregular, ragged holes – and stems – which may be completely or partially severed. They will climb up walls or the sides of pots to obtain their favourite food. Snails will climb up flower stems to reach the flower spike (see **Figure 9.1a**). A silvery slime trail assists you in locating these pests. Obviously, as they feed on decaying vegetable matter, pots and borders should be kept free of weeds and fallen leaves, and

ABOVE: **Figure 9.1a.** Flower spikes and leaves destroyed by snail attack.

comes to these species by the actions of cars, cats and such predators as crows and magpies than from accidentally imbibing these pellets, which are in any case now treated with bitter substances to deter other species from eating them. Slug pellets should never be used in mounds, and the containers should not be left lying around accessible to pets or small children.

Alternative approaches to the problem of controlling slugs and snails include the use of aluminium sulphate solutions, which it is claimed cause shrinkage of the organs used in slime production, and also kill eggs. However, it is necessary to use a large volume at regular intervals to effect any control, and there is a risk of build-up of aluminium in the soil and in run-off to watercourses. Usage in pots may reduce this risk, but could lead to the build-up of acidity in the compost.

Nematodes that specifically target slugs have been introduced as 'biological controls'. These parasites come in a dry clay mix and are kept refrigerated until the soil is warm enough for them to be active, which is about 5°C (41°F). For this reason, in temperate climates they cannot be used during the winter months. In order to use them, water is added to the clay mix and the preparation is evenly distributed over the area to be treated. However, the nematode preparation should not be used on heavy soils and should be kept clear of ponds. The nematodes only survive for six weeks, so this method is probably not sensible for general use in a large garden.

Other less expensive methods include the use of attractants such as grapefruit halves or 'slug pubs' – plastic containers sunk in the ground and filled with beer. These must be periodically renewed and the slugs disposed of. Simply collecting slugs and snails after dark and placing them in a bucket containing a liquid detergent solution is one quite effective but rather time-consuming approach. Perhaps the answer is to move to drier soils, such as those found in some parts of the United States that are slug-free, but since these are mostly desert areas, watering plants becomes a necessity.

edges of borders cleared of overhanging grass, especially in the autumn, to discourage slug migration. During the winter and early spring, crowns of delphinium plants can be covered with a generous handful of coarse sand or grit, which will give some protection to the dormant crown buds.

Probably the most effective control can be obtained by the careful use of proprietary brands of slug pellets, which contain 3 per cent metaldehyde. These blue 'mini' pellets should be used as directed by the manufacturer and spread around precious plants at low density. We have hedgehogs, frogs and numerous song birds in our garden, and feel that more harm

Caterpillars

There is nothing more frustrating than finding many of the florets missing from a promising flower spike. The absence of a slime trail rules out molluscs, but evidence in the form of caterpillar droppings can often be found on leaves, especially if the culprit is already large. Other signs of damage indicating these unwelcome pests are leaves that appear like a folded napkin or a collapsed umbrella because the leaf stalk has been chewed. Small pieces of leaf may be folded over and stitched with silk to protect the caterpillar inside (see **Figure 9.1b**). Much damage arises in early spring from caterpillars that over-winter, either as eggs laid by the adult the previous autumn, or as small individuals in the base of the plant. Cutting down old stems and cleaning up the base of plants in the autumn helps reduce these early attacks.

Tiny dark-green caterpillars with grey spots that hide in the stitched-up leaves can cause considerable damage. These caterpillars change as they grow, becoming paler green with dark green lines down the back and white lines along the lower sides. When ready to pupate, they spin a golden cocoon on the underside of a leaf, which is very visible (see **Figure 9.1c**). These caterpillars are the larvae of the golden plusia (*Polychrysia moneta*), also known as the delphinium moth. The moth is widespread in continental Europe as well as in England, Wales and much of Scotland. It is on the wing during nights in June and July, and is attracted to the nectar of many garden flowers. In the past it was thought that the tiny black-spotted caterpillars in leaf-rolls were the larvae of moths belonging to the family *Tortricidae*, but evidence obtained by growing these caterpillars to maturity showed otherwise.

Other moths with a wide distribution in Europe are the angleshades (*Phlogophora meticulosa*) and the silver Y (*Autographa gamma*). The latter arrive as migrants in the spring. The caterpillars of both these moths are green and have voracious appetites. Larvae of the angleshades pupate on the soil surface in brown cocoons, while

Other Insect Pests

Among other flying pests are aphids, leafhoppers, leafminer flies, thrips and, recently, pollen beetles. The latter move from neighbouring fields of oilseed rape (canola) to flowers in the garden, especially white delphiniums and sweet peas. Whether they transmit any disease is not documented, but they certainly feast on pollen and thus reduce potential yields of seed. They will not be welcome guests on your chosen 'pollen' parents.

Aphids, which belong to the Hemiptera or plant bugs, are important pests in Europe and North America, some being selective feeders, others feeding on all garden plants. Armed with piercing mouthparts forming a structure like a hypodermic needle, they damage and distort the growth of leaves and buds. Plants may harbour winged adults, wingless adults and young. The large quantities of sap excreted gives rise to 'honey dew', which attracts ants and favours the growth of sooty mould. Much more serious is the fact that they transmit viruses from plant to plant during feeding activity. In the UK aphids do not appear to colonize delphiniums, although they will alight and sample the plant as a possible food source, and so can transmit viral particles. In North America the larger rosy aphis (*Anuraphis roseus*) can be troublesome. Any signs of infestation should be treated with a systemic insecticide, but this will not inhibit random sampling and thus potential virus transmission.

Leafhoppers, which have an appearance rather like elongated aphids, are capable of piercing plant cells and sucking up sap. The adults can jump off plants when disturbed and move to another plant, leaving behind damaged areas that give rise to a mottled pattern of coarse yellow or white spots on the leaves. In North America the aster leafhopper (*Macrosteles fascifrons*) transmits a phycoplasma that causes 'aster yellows' in many plants – including delphiniums – for which there is no cure. Any plants that are affected should be burnt.

TOP LEFT: **Figure 9.1b.** Collapsed leaves and pieces of folded leaf indicate caterpillar activity.

BOTTOM LEFT: **Figure 9.1c.** Caterpillar and golden cocoon of the golden plusia or delphinium moth on the underside of a partly eaten delphinium leaf.

ABOVE: **Figure 9.1d.** A caterpillar of the large ranunculus moth mimics a stem as it munches a delphinium flower bud.

those of the silver Y produce white silken cocoons located on the underside of leaves. Both will produce at least two broods of caterpillars each year, but those of the migrant do not usually survive the winters of northern Europe. Another large green caterpillar, which is known to damage delphiniums, is the larva of the large Ranunculus moth, *Polymixis flavicincta* (see **Figure 9.1d**). This moth is widespread in continental Europe from the southern Netherlands to the Mediterranean, but in Britain it only seems to frequent the south. In our 'caterpillar arena' these caterpillars produced peat-covered cocoons from which the adult moths emerged very late in the year.

For those gardeners with a small collection of delphiniums, vigilant removal of caterpillars by hand in early spring will probably be sufficient to control these pests. Growers with a large number of plants or a build-up of moths will need to spray with the appropriate systemic insecticide.

Another group of insect pests that can build up in large numbers are thrips (*Thysanoptera*), often called thunderflies. They also feed by puncturing shoots, leaves, buds and flowers, sucking out the sap so that the cells are drained of their contents. Visible signs of this damage are yellow flecks, which later become brown, and large areas of tissue can become discoloured and distorted. In North America, pear thrips (*Taeniothrips inconsequens*), which ruin buds of maples and azaleas, have also been observed to damage delphiniums early in the season. A serious pest introduced into glasshouses in the UK is the 'western flower thrips', *Frankliniella occidentalis*. This thrips, occurring widely in parts of Europe and North America, transmits the Tomato Spotted Wilt Virus, which has been found in delphiniums.

Another pest that thankfully, at the moment, does not seem to attack our delphiniums, but can be disastrous in North America, is the cyclamen or strawberry mite, *Tarsonemus pallidus*. Tarsonemid mites are very small and are only noticed when damaged plants are found. These mites embed themselves into growing shoots and feed in flower buds, stunting growth and spoiling the flowers. Dormant during cold periods, mites are stimulated by higher temperatures (21–25°C/70–77°F), and breeding is then continuous. Although commercial growers have access to acaricides, no preparations are available to amateurs and the only control is to burn affected shoots and buds. These mites are so small that it is easy to scatter infected material. We may have been lucky because we have had problems with Michaelmas daisies (*Aster novi-belgii*) in some years, although we do not grow strawberries. Maybe these mites are dormant since the critical developmental period of our delphiniums occurs at lower temperatures.

Nematodes

The build up of nematodes (eelworms) in the soil is a further problem that is not easy for amateurs to tackle because soil sterilization is required. These pests invade roots or shoots of plants and lead to distortion and, in severe attacks, loss of the plant. Some nematodes also carry virus particles. These thin, unsegmented worm-like animals, generally less than 1 centimetre (⅜ inch) in length, are not easy to see. They possess a spear-like stylet in the head end that enables them to penetrate plant tissues and suck sap. Reproduction by eggs leads to miniature young that grow rapidly and moult several times.

Delphiniums and many other garden plants are hosts for *Aphelenchoides sp.* which enter the lower leaves and will migrate upwards, being favoured by wet or misty conditions. Under outdoor conditions, where for example dead leaves are the only nutrient source available, these nematodes do not normally survive, but they can do so under glasshouse conditions – for example, on chrysanthemum stools kept for propagation. The common root lesion eelworm, *Pratylenchus sp.*, is a migratory root endoparasite and will invade and feed in root tissues causing necrosis that appears on the surface of the root as brown or black lesions. Other species of nematodes browsing on roots – *Longidorus* and *Xiphinema* have a worldwide distribution – carry viruses such as Raspberry Ring Spot and Strawberry Ring Spot. Note that many common garden weeds are also hosts to these nematodes, and thus their viruses.

Mammals

Among larger pests that a delphinium grower, or any gardener, has to contend with are voles and field mice, moles, foxes, rabbits, squirrels, and in North America, groundhogs and chipmunks as well. Moles and voles are particularly destructive as their tunnels run under and through root masses, either destroying roots or leaving the plant without contact with the underlying soil (see **Figure 9.1e**). Foxes and rabbits also cause root disturbance, but are easier to control by the use of netting. Sadly, trapping is the only way to deal with voles and moles.

ABOVE: **Figure 9.1e.**
Vole activity destroys a promising delphinium seedling.

Mildew

Delphiniums suffer from relatively few diseases, but powdery mildew can disfigure leaves, stems and flower buds. Becoming prevalent during hot, dry periods, mildew can be seen quite early in the UK. Some knowledge of the mildew life cycle can help control the problem.

Powdery mildews are a group of fungi that infect the aerial parts of plants and are dependent on living hosts. They do not directly kill their hosts, but do weaken them. These pathogens are, like their plant hosts, cellular, but they lack chloroplasts and so depend on their hosts for nutrients. Belonging to the family *Erysiphaceae*, they are filamentous and form a mycelium of filaments or hyphae. Together with spores (conidiospores) produced vegetatively by specialized hyphae, this mycelium gives rise to the characteristic whitish-grey 'powder' seen on the leaves and stem of infected plants. There are a large number of mildew species that may be restricted to a family,

genus, species or even variety of a plant host. The powdery mildew that infects *Delphinium sp.* is *Erysiphe ranunculi*, which also infects *Ranunculus, Adonis vernalis* and *Clematis sp.* Leaves can be infected by conidiospores (or ascospores produced after sexual reproduction) arriving on the leaf surface, if there is sufficient humidity to allow germination of the spore. During dry periods, humid conditions are provided by overnight dew formation. Hyphae produced by germinating spores penetrate the cuticle, and the cell wall of host cells, but they do not penetrate the cell membrane. They attach at specialized points (haustoria) through which nutrients can move from the host cell to the fungal cell. *Erysiphe sp.* remain only in the surface layer of the leaf. Growth of fungal hyphae leads to production of large numbers of conidiospores that, when released, cause further infection, especially during dry conditions. At the end of the growing season when plants die down, the fungus enters a sexual phase of activity, producing resistant fruiting bodies (cleistotheca), which contain over-wintering ascospores. These fruiting bodies can remain in dead leaf litter, or other material around plants, and possibly within the scales of dormant crown buds.

The number of effective fungicides still available to amateurs in the UK has been greatly reduced by legislation requiring stringent testing of chemicals to show they are effective and safe for garden use. Products containing either myclobutanil or penconazole should be sought. It is likely, however, that resistance to these fungicides will build up in the pathogen. The old-fashioned treatment with sulphur dust is quite effective in the warm, protected environment of a greenhouse, and even in the outside environment can offer some control to low levels of infection. Clearly, keeping delphinium plants well separated and away from other host species is sensible, but not always achievable. Since wet conditions may reduce spore dispersal, overhead spraying has been recommended during dry periods. With the increasing problem of water shortages in summer, this may not be possible, and one would not wish to spoil any flowers that may be out. Also, it should be remembered that some humidity is required for the spores of *Erysiphe* to germinate. Reducing the number of susceptible cultivars grown could be one approach, since some of the best purples (such as 'Chelsea Star') and deep lavenders (such as 'Gordon Forsyth') are very mildew-prone (see **Figure 9.1f**). Most purples – and indeed most cultivated delphiniums – do suffer towards the end of a dry season. We find that, far from offering a means of introducing resistance to mildew, most species delphiniums that we have grown are actually more vulnerable to this pathogen. One exception appears to be *D. requienii*, but this species is a biennial and not suitable for a conventional breeding programme.

Crown Rots and Related Disorders

Since the early 1930s many delphinium growers in the UK have experienced a type of crown or root rot in which the leaves and stems yellow and the spike dies. The stem can be pulled out of the crown, below which is found a mass of wet, rotting material (see **Figure 9.2a**).

The yellowing and early death of the lower leaves on some plants should not be confused with crown rot. This can be likened to premature ageing, and may be due to drought, impoverished soils or simply lack of sunlight. In this case, the stem is still attached to the crown and the spike continues to grow and expand, and the florets to open normally.

Much effort has been devoted to the problem of crown rot without any definitive answers. Pieces of dying tissue have been plated on to sterile media, but no fungal pathogens have been detected. However, considerable numbers of bacteria of different types were found, though these did not induce any crown or root rot when introduced experimentally into trial delphinium cuttings.

In the United States well-documented and very damaging fungal pathogens, *Sclerotium delphinii* and *Sclerotium rolfsii*, are known to cause rotting of delphinium

TOP LEFT: **Figure 9.1f.**
A purple seedling badly
affected by infection with
powdery mildew.

BOTTOM LEFT: **Figure 9.2a.**
Yellowing leaves and a
rotten stem of a delphinium
dying with crown rot.

BELOW: **Figure 9.2b.**
Multiple shoot growths at
the base of a delphinium in
July suggest the presence
of leafy gall.

crowns. These are nectotrophic fungi, which can live as saphrophytes in the soil or decaying matter. They are not specialized and can only enter their hosts through wounds or other openings. On entering, they produce hyphae that spread rapidly, killing host tissues and then feeding saprophytically on the dead cells. They are not host-specific. Sclerotia, reddish-brown in colour, form in the mycelium of hyphae located in the dying host. These sclerotia spread the disease to other plants so that control can only be achieved by the removal of the entire root ball of the plant and the adjacent soil. This pathogen survives in warm, sub-tropical regions of the United States and other similar regions of the world, but is unable to survive cold winters. Although it is not found further north in North America, it persists as a

reservoir in warmer areas from which it can spread northwards on any contaminated plant material.

A number of soft rots are caused by pathogenic bacteria and may gain entry through cut surfaces, natural openings such as stomata or wounding due to nematode activity. The host tissue often dies in localized areas and becomes brown, for example giving rise to spots on leaves. One common cause of 'black spots' on delphinium leaves, particularly in the spring, arises from infection with *Pseudomonas syringae* pv. *delphinii*. These bacteria require wet conditions in order to spread, and splash from ground level is the reason why it is the lower leaves that become infected. Whether like *Erwinia amylovora* (the causative agent of fireblight in some members of the *Rosaceae*) the spread of these bacteria down stems is partly responsible for the early stages of crown rot is debatable, but there is no evidence to support this possibility.

Leafy gall, caused by the activity of the bacterium *Rhodococcus fasciens* (*Corynebacterium fasciens*) may occur in a wide range of ornamental plants in northern Europe and North America. This rod-shaped, gram-positive bacterium can live from season to season in the soil. The infected plant can be recognized by an abnormally large number of short shoots at the basal region, and these are often thickened and distorted. In culture, the bacterium does not grow at temperatures below 7°C (45°F) or above 35°C (95°F), which would suggest that it is not active during the colder months of the year. There is no cure for this infection and soil disinfection is only sensible in small areas such as glasshouses. The activity of this bacterium leads to overstimulation of shoot production in normally dormant crown material, which can lead to a general weakening of the plant (see **Figure 9.2b**). In strawberries, the so-called 'cauliflower disease' is a result of some strains of the bacterium being carried into the plants by the nematode *Aphelenchoides ritzemabosi*. This nematode has many hosts, including delphiniums.

Fasciation

Whether another malformation of delphinium stems, known as fasciation, can be linked to leafy gall is unclear. Fasciation includes gross flattening of the flower spike, stem division leading to multiple spike formation, and 'whiskering', in which florets are replaced by leaf bracts (see **Figure 9.2c**). The formation of the flower stems occurs very early in the season, shortly after the shoots have grown above ground level. Changes in temperature at this time of year, such as overnight frost, could interfere with the many cell divisions taking place in the growing shoots and result in growth abnormalities. It is not normally necessary to dispose of a delphinium that produces fasciated stems only occasionally, but if it does so regularly it should be discarded.

ABOVE: **Figure 9.2c.** Two fasciated, flattened delphinium stems.

Viral Diseases

The presence of viruses in plants is difficult to determine unless the effects are so extreme that plants are considerably distorted or die from cell lesions. Viruses are obligate parasites and can only multiply after gaining entry into the cells of the host plant. Invisible except under the electron microscope, viruses that infect plants generally have genetic information carried by RNA (ribonucleic acid), though a few do possess DNA, packaged in a protective protein coat or shell called a capsid. Plant viruses are named after the disease symptom they cause in their host and after the host plant in which it was first found, even if that plant is not economically important. Generally, an acronym of the initial letters designate a virus once the full name has been established. Probably the most familiar to gardeners are the Tobacco Mosaic Virus (TMV) and the Cucumber Mosaic Virus (CMV). Cauliflower Mosaic Virus, with the same initials as the previous example, is shortened to CaMV.

Viruses are normally only able to enter the plant host through a wound, most frequently when an insect vector such as an aphid lands on a leaf surface and starts to feed by inserting probing mouthparts. Some viruses are able to enter leaf cells through small abrasions on the surface due to damage caused by neighbouring leaves rubbing in the wind, or by animal interference. The initial entry of the virus (primary infection) may be limited to local loss of chlorophyll (chlorosis) leading to yellowing or to death of cells (necrosis). The virus is usually able to spread to the vascular system and thus, potentially, throughout the plant, causing a secondary or systemic infection.

Stunting of growth is a common consequence of virus infection, but may be a difficult symptom to observe especially if the gardener has only one plant of the cultivar. More obvious symptoms include 'mosaics' (chlorotic patches on leaves) and 'ring-spotting' (in which an area of normal green colour surrounded by a ring, or broken ring, of chlorotic cells; see **Figure 9.2d**). Distortion of the leaves so that they are reduced in area or become strap-like in form, along with changes to flower form – particularly streaking or flecking of the colour – are relatively easy symptoms to notice (see **Figures 9.2e and f**). The

RIGHT: **Figure 9.2d.**
A pattern of chlorotic cells (ring spotting) in the leaves of a lavender seedling suggest a viral infection.

ABOVE: **Figure 9.2e.**
The normal florets of a selected lavender seedling.

RIGHT: **Figure 9.2f.**
Dramatic changes in the form of florets of a selected lavender seedling, coupled with ring spotting in the leaves (see **Figure 9.2d**) indicate severe viral infection.

problem is that these symptoms may also be due to damage by hormone weedkillers or other agrochemicals. Leaf mosaics may just be due to natural leaf variegation or the lack of certain trace elements.

Often plants infected by a virus show no visible external symptoms and they are said to show 'latent infection'. Many infected wild plants, for example chickweed (*Stellaria media*), are overwintering hosts for CMV, as are shrubs such as privet, honeysuckle and buddleia. The existence of these tolerant plants is probably the consequence of natural selection, and it is likely that generations of gardeners have also selected (whether knowingly or not) for tolerant cultivars.

The virus that most frequently infects *Delphinium sp.*, as well as a very wide range of flowering plants, is probably CMV, which is readily transmitted by a number of aphids, including the common greenfly and the peach potato aphid. Although we have said that aphids do not generally colonize delphiniums, the winged forms, especially in mid-summer, alight on leaves and sample sap using their stylet mouthparts. Since they generally find delphiniums not to their liking, the winged aphids move off to another plant, whether another delphinium or a herbaceous neighbour. Unfortunately, aphids transmit CMV in a manner that is termed 'non-persistent'. Aphids acquire the virus particles by probing an infected plant, then they move on, probe a neighbouring plant and release these virus particles into it. Viral particles do not remain in the aphid over a long period and do not multiply within the insect, so viruses are acquired and passed on within a very short period. Often symptoms of the infection never show up during periods of fast growth, but instead are seen at times of the year when temperatures are low, or on old leaves.

Work in 1975 by K W Bailiss looking at viral infections in delphiniums also showed the presence of another virus, Broad Bean Wilt Virus (BBWV), which is transmitted by aphids in a non-persistent manner. He noted that when CMV and BBWV were both present, delphinium leaves were distorted, excessively dissected and the growth of the plant stunted. It seems possible that the most severe symptoms seen in delphiniums are due to the synergistic effect of both viruses.

Tomato Spotted Wilt Virus (TSWV), which causes severe necrotic symptoms and losses of ornamental crops grown under glass, has also been found in delphiniums. Outbreaks in this country have been associated with the western flower thrips (*Frankliniella occidentalis*), which until recently was only found in North America.

Some viruses transmitted by nematodes from certain genera (*Longidorus and Xiphinema*), are persistent in their nematode hosts. These include Raspberry Ring Spot (RRSV) and Strawberry Latent Ring Spot (SLRV), which have a wide range of hosts, including chickweed and *Viola tricolor*. Both these viruses have been reported in delphiniums.

Clearly there is rather little the gardener can do to avoid some viral infection in plants, and if the symptoms are not severe then we have to live with them. A programme of eradication followed by introducing clean plants would be of little value, since Bailiss has reported that new seedlings could become infected in as little as six weeks. It is clear that the need to reduce the viral burden in the surrounding weed population is very important, as is the control of vectors in the garden. Additionally, the sterilization of knives used in taking cuttings, cutting flower spikes and general maintenance is very important.

10. Hybridizing Delphiniums

Since no two delphinium seedlings are alike in every detail, there is always a sense of anticipation when new plants flower for the first time. This is particularly true if the seedlings result from a hand-cross that you have made. To reach this stage, however, you need already to have succeeded in making a cross, and this chapter describes the steps involved in the process.

The first decision to be made is which cultivars will be used as the parents. Some of the factors influencing this choice have been discussed in chapter 4 but there are a few practical points to remember. One is deciding which plant to use as the seed parent, and it is generally advisable to select the cultivar that reliably sets a good quantity of seed. The second point is that if a large number of seeds are required, supplies of pollen must be available over a considerable period.

If your crossing programme will involve plants in the open ground, make sure they have been adequately fed and watered, and are staked securely. There is nothing more disheartening than finding all your efforts undone by a howling gale. Try to make sure that your chosen plants are readily accessible and that you are not trampling

other treasured plants underfoot (especially if they belong to your co-gardener!). It is fine to use laterals if you do not want too many seeds or do not want to spoil the appearance of the main bloom as a particular garden feature.

It can be more efficient to use plants growing in pots for both seed and pollen parents. Like delphiniums in the open ground, these pot-grown plants must be well looked after (see chapter 8). The advantage is that the plants are mobile and can be moved to a sheltered position if rain threatens. Alternatively, the pots can be taken into a greenhouse, preferably of adequate height to allow air to circulate above the plants, giving a much more comfortable environment for the pollinator. Also, if the plants are put into the greenhouse at an earlier stage of growth, hand-pollination can commence much sooner than outside in the garden. It is preferable to hand-pollinate during the main flowering season, allowing six weeks at this time of the year for the seed to develop and ripen. It is also possible to use flowers late in the summer, especially under cover, but it is not sensible to continue into the autumn as development slows down and the seed needs time to ripen. The production of a mature seed requires the development of the embryo and the laying down of food reserves (the endosperm). The latter involves a complex process of shutting down enzyme activity, which must be completed to produce a viable seed for storage.

The chosen seed parent is carefully watched for the opening of the lower florets. As soon as a floret starts to open, the coloured sepals are removed carefully, as are the petals, including the nectary (see **Figure 10.1a**). Some people leave the sepals intact and only remove the petals but, having observed bees visiting flowers prepared in this way, we prefer to err on the

Figure 10.1. Steps in making a hand cross.

RIGHT: **Figure 10.1a.** Removing sepals reveals the petals and anthers.

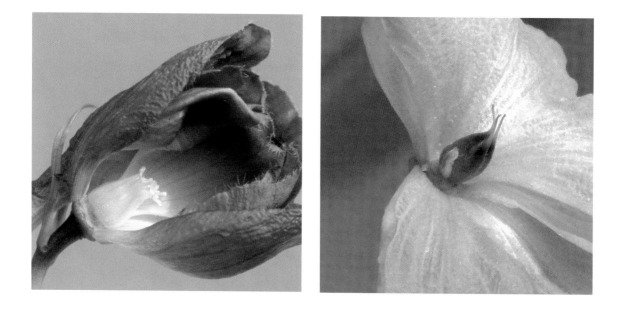

side of caution and remove all this material so insects are no longer attracted to the flower. We remove the anthers at this time by carefully snipping or rubbing them off between the fingers. This is to ensure that they are removed before they have a chance to split open and release pollen grains (see **Figure 10.1b**). In a few cultivars, the anthers start to split open very early and, for these plants, the sepals should be removed as early as possible. The prepared floret or florets are labelled, and on successive days more florets are prepared; this procedure is termed emasculation.

At this point, the stigmas of the female part of the flower are still tucked away and are not obvious. They are not damaged by careful emasculation and may take from three to four days to become visible and receptive to pollen. Stigma development is dependent on temperature, so may occur much more quickly in very hot weather. Cultivars vary in the timing of stigma receptivity, some being receptive much sooner than others. At first the stigma is a hook-shaped structure, but it turns upwards and the tip opens to form an inverted V-shape (see **Figure 10.1c**). The stigma is fully receptive when sticky mucus can be seen, although this is not easy to detect; the V-shape is a useful alternative indicator of receptivity. Dry pollen grains are collected from the prospective 'father' using a clean, fine artist's brush that is slightly moistened (see **Figure 10.1d**). Pollen is collected from freshly opened anthers and transferred to the waiting stigma. We prefer this method, rather than removing a whole floret as the pollen source, because it avoids any contamination of the stigma by foreign pollen grains within the floret. The brush, with its load of visible pollen grains, is gently stroked over the stigmas of the prepared florets (see **Figure 10.1e**). If a stigma is truly receptive, many thousands of pollen grains will stick on its surface. Since one cannot really tell if the stigma is 'just right', pollination is repeated on a further two days.

The ovaries begin to swell up quite rapidly if fertilization has occurred and, if there are no incompatibility problems, your task is done. It must be mentioned that there are instances when the pods apparently swell up but no seeds are produced, for example when working with cream or purple cultivars; we call this a 'false pregnancy'.

Pollination, whether of a few florets or a whole spike, continues in a sequential way until you have completed your task. The seed parent is left to allow the seeds to

ABOVE LEFT: **Figure 10.1b.** Removing the anthers before they open to shed pollen grains has emasculated the flower.

ABOVE RIGHT: **Figure 10.1c.** Receptive stigmas awaiting pollen grains.

ABOVE LEFT: **Figure 10.1d.** Pollen is collected using an artist's brush.

ABOVE RIGHT: **Figure 10.1e.** Transferring pollen grains to the receptive stigmas.

ABOVE: **Figure 10.1f.** Seed pods ready for harvesting.

mature and ripen. This may take five to six weeks in the UK, and careful attention to watering is still required. We do not cover the developing seed pods because damp conditions lead to the growth of moulds. Vigilance is required because caterpillars and earwigs may climb the stems and damage seed pods; smearing a small quantity of Vaseline around the stem should inhibit this mountaineering activity. Bullfinches, although beautiful birds, are very partial to delphinium seeds and damage the seed pods just before the seeds are ripe. They slice open the pods and peck out the seeds with seemingly no toxic effect. All these pests are a good reason for pollinating more florets than you need because your valuable F1 seeds can be lost in many ways, and a whole year's work is then wasted.

Seeds should be harvested just before the seed pod splits open naturally and exposes them to fungal spores in the environment. To test if seeds are ripe enough, squeeze the pods gently to see whether the pod splits open (see **Figure 10.1f**). The pod is cut off if it opens under gentle pressure. At this time, the seed is dark-coloured with a fully developed seed coat but it is still moist and needs further drying to maintain viability in storage.

After collection, seed pods are placed in labelled, open containers (sandwich boxes or ice cream tubs are useful) for this final drying in a cool place. The pods split open and release their seeds into the container. The seeds should be separated from undeveloped ovules, any white immature seeds and pod fragments. Store seeds in labelled 'Glassine' envelopes, like those used by stamp collectors. Alternatively, plastic 'Grippa' bags will serve, though the seeds become attracted to the sides of the bag by a static charge, making them less easy to retrieve. The envelopes are placed in screw-top jars or more sandwich boxes and stored in a domestic refrigerator at around 4°C (39°F). In this way viability is retained over a long period. We have obtained germination in some cases even after seed has been stored for 18 years, although the viability is reduced over time and the seed takes far longer to reactivate.

The average yield of hand-pollinated seed per whole spike pollinated depends on the cultivars used and the weather conditions. Provided the pollen parent is fertile and there are no incompatibility problems, one can expect around 700–1,000 seeds per average-length spike. As mentioned previously, pods are sometimes virtually empty, in which case only 150 seeds may be obtained per spike.

Collection of open-pollinated seed should follow the same procedure. We carefully harvest pods just before opening and place them on large open trays to dry. We prefer this to collecting whole spikes and hanging them up to dry, as the seed is freer from contaminants such as caterpillars, and less of it is unripe. Large quantities of seed need to be sieved and 'blown' to remove lightweight unfertilized seed and broken pieces of pod. It is worthwhile spending some time carefully picking over the seed by hand to remove mouldy seeds or other contaminants before storing in labelled jars at the bottom of the refrigerator.

11. Growing Species

The activities of delphinium breeders have given us a range of colour and form in garden delphiniums derived from *D. elatum*. Over a considerably longer time Nature has achieved great diversity of colour and form within the genus and within each species. This diversity is maintained by factors such as geographical isolation and variation in flowering period, but few of us have the opportunity to share the beauty of the flowers by travelling to the regions where the plants grow indigenously. However, we can enjoy them in our gardens by growing some of the species from seed.

Species delphiniums are not difficult to grow from seed so long as one tries to understand the problems of their natural environment. Many delphiniums are found in mountainous areas, where they grow in poor soils or in leaf detritus between rocks. Often under snow cover for many months of the year, they produce leaves, flowers and seeds in a relatively short period after snow melt and before high temperatures or drought induce dormancy. To survive under these circumstances their rootstock is much modified and often tuberous, and seeds often have special germination requirements.

Some Easily Grown Species

It is best to start by growing some of the less demanding species, which will germinate readily at temperatures around 15–17°C (59–63°F) when sown early in the year. Into this category fall the red-flowered *D. cardinale* and *D. nudicaule*, the blue *D. grandiflorum* v. *chinense* and *D. ceratophorum* and the blue-lavender *D. cashmerianum* (see **Figure 11.1**). Some of these are often grown as half-hardy annuals, but all are perennial and will survive in well-drained sites such as rock gardens or tubs. Both of the red delphiniums need to be sown early in good-quality compost to give flowering-sized plants in mid-summer. On germination, *D. cardinale* produces two separate cotyledons, with the true leaves being produced between them. *D. nudicaule* differs and produces a single stalk bearing two fused cotyledons at the apex, while the first true leaves arise from a small tuber below ground around two to three weeks later. Both species tolerate pricking out, but this should not be attempted until true leaves are present. Grow them in 9-centimetre (3½-inch) pots until a number of leaves are present before planting out. The smaller *D. nudicaule* will grow best in a rock garden, or as an edging to a large tub, while *D. cardinale* is better in the open ground near the front of a border where the scarlet well-separated

BELOW: **Figure 11.1.** The hooded flowers of *D. cashmerianum* make an attractive plant at the edge of a border.

LEFT: **Figure 11.2.**
The scarlet flowers on spikes of *D. cardinale* can offer you a display of strong colour in your summer borders.

florets will give a dramatic plant (see **Figure 11.2**). Support these species using twiggy sticks, as the junction between the stems and crown is weak. If the plants are too small, they will not flower in the first season, but instead go dormant. The next season for them starts early (in the UK), after November rainfall, when the leaves appear and they are at risk in cold weather.

The golden larkspur, *Delphinium luteum*, once found along the coast of Sonoma County in California, is an endangered species now known only from two wild populations in Bodega Bay and North Marin County. However, some seed from cultivated plants is often available and is worth growing, both to increase the stock and to enjoy the beautiful flowers. Like seed of the red delphiniums, this germinates without problems, and the cotyledons are produced at the apex of one stalk. The true leaves arise from below the compost surface after about three weeks – like *D. nudicaule*, which it resembles. Both species have fleshy leaves, and the branching stalks bear 5–25 florets in an open pyramid. The florets open to reveal bright-yellow sepals that have a waxy appearance and yellow petals (see **Figure 11.3**). Plants may reach flowering size from an early sowing, but they will flower in April or early May in following years.

D. luteum is best grown in pots so that water can be withheld during the dormant period. Thought by some authorities to be either a variant of *D. nudicaule* or possibly of hybrid origin, recent work suggests that neither of these assumptions is correct. The sepals of the rare yellow variant of *D. nudicaule* are a flat, rather dull colour when compared with those of *D. luteum*. If you are lucky enough to grow this species, it is worth keeping the plants of *D. luteum* separate from any other species flowering at the same time. To ensure that you will have more seeds to grow, carry out some hand-pollination, as *D. luteum* sets seed very readily.

RIGHT: **Figure 11.3.** Bright yellow flowers of *D. luteum* glisten in the spring sunshine on a plant growing in the greenhouse.

Some More Challenging Species

A very large number of species delphiniums come from areas where winters are hard and unfavourable to plant growth. It is therefore not surprising that certain conditions have to be met before seeds will germinate. Seeds germinating just before the onset of winter will not survive. Such seeds require a cold, wet period ranging from three weeks to four or five months to occur before germination. This is frequently found with plants of alpine origin, and the usual approach is to leave the seeds outside during the winter months after sowing in pots of good-quality compost. These pots should be placed in trays covered with lids of small mesh wire netting to prevent mice from eating them (see **Figure 11.4**). Sadly, it is all too easy to lose seeds in this way, even the first evening after sowing! The disadvantage of this approach is that in many parts of the UK winters are never continuously cold. Periods of colder weather are interspersed with milder weather, so for many species the length of chilling is not sufficient for germination.

Another method to use involves 'chitting' and the refrigerator. Wet paper kitchen towel (plain white and not the decorated variety, which contains unwanted dyes) is placed on the bottom of a small container that can be closed with a lid. Seeds are spaced out over this area, then covered with another piece of wet paper towel, and the lid, labelled with the species (use an indelible pen) is fitted on top. Place these containers in a domestic refrigerator in which the temperature should be around 4°C (39°F). Some species require such a long period of treatment that it is a good idea to put the container in a plastic bag to lessen water loss during this time. Growing a lot of species seeds in this way takes up a considerable volume of refrigerator space, which can lead to domestic conflict! If possible, therefore, it is ideal to keep a dedicated refrigerator for chilling seeds, which has the additional advantage that the less frequently the door is opened the more constant the temperature will be. This

dedicated unit can also store containers of dry seeds over long periods of time (see chapter 10).

After about three weeks, and at weekly intervals thereafter, containers of chilled seeds need to be checked to see whether germination has commenced. When a root has emerged each seed is transferred into individual 5-centimetre (2-inch) pots of moist compost, using a pair of tweezers. Very few species will show simultaneous germination, and the container should be returned to the refrigerator as soon as possible. Place the small pots into a tray with a domed plastic cover to retain adequate moisture, and leave until the cotyledons emerge. Seedlings should be transferred to adequate light and treated as for other delphiniums (see chapter 7). Using this method, the viability of the seed can be ascertained and the need for pricking out has been eliminated. Many species delphiniums will *not* tolerate root disturbance. When needed, plants can be potted up progressively with minimal disturbance. Many unusual delphiniums can be grown successfully using this simple method.

ABOVE: **Figure 11.4.** Pots of seed need to be covered by a wire-mesh lid when left outside in the garden during winter, to protect them from the attentions of mice.

D. semibarbatum

You might be surprised to find that *D. semibarbatum* requires three weeks of cold, wet conditions before it will germinate. Although it comes from Iran, it is indigenous to the high, mountainous areas of that country, not the sun-baked lowlands, and flowering occurs before the hot dry summer, with growth recommencing after winter rain. The small greyish-scaled seeds produce plants with normal cotyledons, and the first true leaves are tri-lobed and very dissected. These seedlings strongly resent root disturbance. Unless started very early, seedlings only produce basal leaves in the first season, and together with increasing day-length and the occurrence of hot, dry weather, the leaves will suddenly turn yellow and die. Watering *must* cease, and all signs of plant life will disappear. Investigation of a pot at this stage will reveal a small, chubby rootstock (see **Figure 11.5a**). The following spring, after a modest quantity of water, new leaves will arise from the rootstock (**Figure 11.5b**), and eventually, in about June, a flowering stem with numerous laterals will develop. Unlike many delphiniums, the flower buds appear to develop together up the length of the stem and come out almost simultaneously. This flowering stem with its dramatic yellow flowers is quite long-lasting in the garden, and the flowers are good for cutting (see **Figure 11.5c**).

Figure 11.5.
D. semibarbatum.

ABOVE: **Figure 11.5a.**
The chubby rootstocks of young seedlings of *D. semibarbatum.*

RIGHT: **Figure 11.5b.**
Fresh leafy growth of *D. semibarbatum* in spring.

FAR RIGHT: **Figure 11.5c.**
Flowering stems of *D. semibarbatum* in a border give a dramatic yellow splash in August.

D. trolliifolium

A spring-flowering delphinium of wet woodlands in the Columbia River Gorge region of Oregon and Washington states, *D. trolliifolium* (grown from seed collected under licence) has been very successful in our garden. It is also found along the western side of the Cascade Range in Oregon and the northern coastal range of California. Although we find that self-sown seeds will germinate in the soil during the winter months, or if left outside in small pots, the seed does benefit from a short period – three to four weeks – of cold, wet treatment in the refrigerator. Like many of the American species delphiniums, *D. trolliifolium* has a tuberous root, and the sequence of development differs from that of garden hybrids. The cotyledons produced by the germinating seed arise at the top of a single stem that grows to around 3 centimetres (1¼ inches) in height and persists for several weeks. Below ground the root extends, and a tuberous swelling develops just below the soil surface. Sometimes one or two divided true leaves grow from the top of the tuber after four or five weeks, but often seedlings lapse into dormancy before any appear. *No attempt should be made to prick out or disturb seedlings in this first year*, and pots should be kept dry from June until late autumn (see **Figure 11.6a**). Growth will recommence after pots become moist and, in early spring, seedlings should be pricked out when the true leaves begin to emerge.

Any older seedlings with large tubers can be potted into 10-centimetre (4-inch) pots and placed in a cold frame, where these second-year seedlings soon make active root growth, at which point the pot size can be increased again to 1 litre. Plants with a basal rosette of more than four leaves are the most likely to develop a flower stem and to flower in April or May. This stem may grow to 60–90 centimetres (24–35 inches) with around ten florets and should be supported with a small cane. As *D. trolliifolium* grows well in the open ground, even in clay, older seedlings (preferably when they reach the beginning of their third year) can be planted out from pots in early March when conditions permit. Place sharp sand or grit around the crown, and use slug deterrent. Over subsequent years, plants may grow multiple stems and bear 20 or more bright-blue florets, each with a dramatic white eye (see **Figure 11.6b**). Remember to support the stems with twiggy sticks or canes to prevent breakage of the plant at the crown. After flowering, the foliage withers and plants become dormant, even during wet periods in the summer months.

ABOVE: **Figure 11.6b.** Multiple flower stems from mature plants of *D. trolliifolium* give colour in the garden during early April.

LEFT: **Figure 11.6a.** Tubers of second-year seedlings of *D. trolliifolium*, together with newly germinated seedlings.

D. variegatum

An attractive dwarf delphinium, *D. variegatum* (or the Royal Larkspur) is a species that we think merits being widely grown. Described in the *Flora of North America* as 'one of the most commonly encountered plants in California, at times colouring foothills of the Coast Ranges and the Sierra Nevada', this delphinium is a plant that flowers in the spring in grassland and open oak woodland. Generally there are fewer than ten deep-royal-blue florets per flower spike, but with significant variation between populations in relation to flower size; some forms have exceptionally large flowers. A number of previous writers on delphiniums have mentioned this species by an older name, *D. emiliae*, and have compared it with the Chinese *D. grandiflorum*. Unlike the latter, however, we are not aware of the use of *D. variegatum* in cultivation, although we feel that it has considerable merit.

Seed, which we sowed in peat-based compost at the beginning of February and left outside in a mix of frosty nights and wet spells, germinated during March. Comparable results were obtained by wet,

cold treatment in the refrigerator, as roots began to emerge after five weeks and germination continued over the following three weeks. Seedlings are exceptionally small, with narrow cotyledons on separate stalks, and the true leaves appear after four weeks (see **Figure 11.7a**). Moved into 9-centimetre (3½-inch) pots in late April, the plants grew very slowly and remained small, with a basal rosette of dissected leaves that by the end of July scarcely overlapped the edges of their pots (see **Figure 11.7b**). It appeared likely that these plants would become dormant until the following spring. However, several were stimulated to flower by the rain from a thunderstorm, which soaked the pots. These plants produced spikes of 8 florets in deep inky-blue tinged with purple, with white upper and blue lateral petals (see **Figure 11.7c**). *D. variegatum* should be kept under relatively dry conditions in a cold frame during the winter, since dormancy is rather easily broken for this species. Mature plants will flower in late spring.

Figure 11.7. Development of *D. variegatum:*

ABOVE: **Figure 11.7a.** Seedlings of *D. variegatum* emerging in late March are very small.

ABOVE: **Figure 11.7b.** Basal rosettes of leaves of *D. variegatum* seedlings in late July.

LEFT: **Figure 11.7c.** The first flowering spike of eight florets, produced in late August.

D. maackianum

Another interesting species from north-eastern China, adjacent regions of Korea and Asiatic Russia is *D. maackianum*, a plant from forest margins and grassy slopes at altitudes of 600–900 metres (2,000–3,000 feet). This hairy plant – with greyish, felt-like leaves and deep-blue flowers with purple bracts – is a fascinating delphinium. Seed sown in mid-January in 9-centimetre (3½-inch) pots was left outdoors, and germination commenced in late March. The seedlings were hairy, with round fleshy cotyledons. After developing a true leaf, seedlings were pricked out in late April and grown in a cold frame. Large, undivided leaves, with only shallow incisions between their lobes, formed a basal rosette. Planted into the open ground in June, these leaves became thick and fleshy, but no sign of any flowering stems could be seen until mid-August. The leaves on these stems, when they appeared, were much more divided, and a most unusual feature (at least in our experience) was the appearance of the brush (collection of young florets). The florets were sheathed by large, purplish-brown leafy bracts to give the appearance of a ball, and these bracts remained a significant feature as the stem expanded and the dark-blue flower buds emerged (see **Figure 11.8**). The mature bloom bore quite large and widely spaced deep-violet-blue florets with a black eye. The bracts were now less significant, and all stems and flowers were extremely hairy. The one disappointing feature of this species is its extreme susceptibility to powdery mildew, so that a regime of fungicide treatment must be employed.

D. hesperium, D. hansenii and D. parryi

Three delphiniums from California, *D. hesperium*, *D. hansenii* and *D. parryi*, display diversity of colour within their species and are relatively easy to grow. All of these species require a continuous cold and wet treatment of four weeks duration, which is most reliably achieved in the refrigerator. Chitting seed of these species has the added advantage of avoiding root disturbance during pricking out. During

their first year of growth, the seedlings produce only leaves and die down early, in June or July. We find that for survival as dormant plants it is important that they grow to a sufficiently large size and, for this reason, we try to start the period of cold, wet treatment in early January. During dormancy they must remain dry, so we keep them under cover until spring. In early February of the second and subsequent years, the pots are fully saturated by placing

ABOVE: **Figure 11.8.** Large purple-brown leafy bracts surround flower buds of *D. maackianum*.

them in trays of water until the compost is thoroughly rehydrated. The pots are then removed from the water but kept moist, and in mid-March a basal rosette of new leaves appears from the surviving plants.

D. hesperium occurs as 3 subspecies, *hesperium* subsp. *hesperium*, *hesperium* subsp. *pallescens* and *hesperium* subsp. *cuyamaceae*, the latter being uncommon and very local in distribution. *D. hesperium* subsp. *hesperium* produces a rosette of lower leaves that are lobed, with smooth upper surfaces, and lower surfaces with prominent veins and numerous little hairs giving a greyish appearance. Plants flourish during a short growing season and produce a flowering stem in May; meanwhile the lower leaves wither and die, which is disconcerting but normal. The individual pale-purple-blue florets are small – 1 centimetre (⅜ inch) across – with a slightly longer spur, and are arranged as a raceme on a downy stem of 45–60 centimetres (18–24 inches). This subspecies is found in open oak woodland with heavy clay soils in northern California, on the western slopes of the northern Coastal Ranges up to 1,100 metres (3,600 feet).

Considered sufficiently different to be placed in another subspecies, *hesperium* subsp. *pallescens* looks very similar until the flowering spike is produced. The flowering stem is smooth, and our plants were shorter than the other subspecies at 40–45 centimetres (16–18 inches), with fewer florets, which were in a delightful pink or pinkish lavender. In another wild collection, the florets were white. Again growing in open oak woodlands, populations of this subspecies are found in the northern Sacramento valley, the Cascade foothills and the Inner Coastal Range, but only on the eastern side of the Coastal Range divide. It is this geographical separation which helps to maintain the two subspecies, since both are diploid (2n=16) and would readily hybridize.

A further and later-flowering subspecies, *hesperium* subsp. *cuyamaceae*, is very restricted in distribution to the region around Lake Cuyamaca (further south than the other subspecies) where it grows on *chapparal*-covered slopes at the edges of pine woods. These are shorter, more compact plants, producing a flowering stem less than 35 centimetres (14 inches). Florets are dark blue with white edging to the upper petals, and differ from the other subspecies in that the basal leaves are still present during flowering.

Often confused with *D. hesperium*, *D. hansenii* is also only found in California. Flowering at the same time, during May, plants of *D. hansenii* produce a denser spike of rather smaller florets on extremely hairy stems. A distinguishing feature, never mentioned in the *Flora*, is that the early rosette of basal leaves in *D. hansenii* shows distinct chocolate blotches that we have never seen in plants of *D. hesperium*. As the leaves grow, these blotches disappear. Just as the flowering stems are very hairy, the leaves bear long hairs, giving them a greyish hue. Once again the basal leaves wither and have almost disappeared by flowering time. Three subspecies of *D. hansenii* have been recognized, one of them, *hansenii* subsp. *ewanianum*, which has dark maroon to reddish-purple flowers, being very local and almost extinct.

Colonies of *hansenii* subsp. *hansenii* grow in clay soils of open oak woodlands throughout the foothills of the Sierra Nevada and the Cascades to about 3,000 metres (10,000 feet), and also in the Sacramento valley. They flower over a long period from May to July, and you will get a range of colours from dark purple-blue through lilac pinks, silvery pinks and white, depending on the colony from which the seed was collected. We find the pinkish forms most attractive. Although diploid, some tetraploid forms have been reported, which could provide very useful material.

Growing in drier conditions in open oak woodland and chaparral, another subspecies, *hansenii* subsp. *kernense*, is found in the Tehachapi Mountains and the southern Sierra Nevada up to 1,900 metres (6,200 feet). This plant is taller, up to 90 centimetres (35 inches), and has a more open spike. The basal leaves, although withered at flowering time, are still present at the base of the spike. In this subspecies the florets are dark blue, although occasional white forms are found. Tetraploid individuals are said to exist.

A species with a wider range than the two previous delphiniums is *D. parryi*. This grows in the drier, sandier soils from San Francisco south to Baja County and inland from these regions, in *chapparal* and open woodlands. There are considered to be sufficiently different forms of this species to warrant subdivision into five subspecies, many of which are extremely local in distribution. The most common subspecies, *parryi* subsp. *parryi*, is a plant growing 45–60 centimetres (18–24 inches) high with palmately lobed basal leaves, which have disappeared by flowering time. The florets are borne on short pedicels held at 45° to the stem, giving a narrow raceme of outward-facing, closely spaced flowers with spreading sepals that reflex with age. The sepals are dark blue, while petals are pale purple. This subspecies is found in the Coastal Ranges on rocky embankments in *chapparal*.

To the east of this, subspecies *parryi* subsp. *purpureum* can be found in drier and colder conditions at the edge of pine woods. In this form, the sepals are a deep blue-purple colour in dense spikes with reflexing sepals (see **Figure 11.9**). The basal leaves are still present at flowering. The other localized subspecies flower in paler blues, greyish blues and whites, but we have not been able to obtain any seeds as yet. We have not found *D. parryi* difficult to grow, and it deserves a spot in a rock garden or tub with sandy, sharply draining soil.

D. recurvatum

A delphinium that comes from the San Joaquin Valley, to the north of Santa Barbara in California, is *D. recurvatum*, the valley larkspur. After sowing in compost at the end of January and leaving the pot outside, germination occurred after about five weeks, and similar results were obtained by leaving the seeds to undergo wet, cold conditions in the refrigerator. From the midpoint of two fleshy cotyledons, trilobed true leaves appeared

LEFT: **Figure 11.9.**
The narrow flowering stem of *D. parryi* subsp. *purpureum* with outwardly facing florets and spreading, reflexing sepals.

Figure 11.10. Development of *D. recurvatum*.

RIGHT: **Figure 11.10a.** The reddish stem of *D. recurvatum* emerging in mid-June.

BELOW: **Figure 11.10b.** Multiple stems from the main stem of *D. recurvatum* increase the number of flowers produced by this attractive plant.

BELOW RIGHT: **Figure 11.10c.** Pinkish-lilac florets of *D. recurvatum* reflex with age.

about six weeks later, and seedlings grew a basal rosette of lobed leaves on very long stalks after a further month. Plants were placed in the open ground, adjacent to our other delphinium seedlings. By mid-June, a reddish-brown flowering stem was produced, accompanied by a number of side shoots from the basal region (see **Figures 11.10a** and **b**). The florets developed simultaneously on the main stem and the side shoots, very different from garden hybrids. Like so many of these American delphiniums, the basal leaves withered and disappeared. The florets were quite large for species delphiniums and the sepals were distinctly veined, reflexing as they opened. We had a variety of colours from pale pink to deep lilac, contrasting with reddish thick stems (see **Figure 11.10c**).

D. californicum

Another delphinium growing in the San Joaquin Valley, but very local in distribution, is *D. californicum* subsp. *interius*, the Hospital Canyon larkspur. Again endemic to California, this delphinium grows on inland-facing open wooded slopes near the coast, while the more common, and very hairy, subspecies *californicum* subsp. *californicum* is a plant of the coastward-facing, often fog-bound slopes from Sonoma County to Santa Barbara County. Seeds of *D. californicum* subsp. *interius* will germinate if sown in pots and left outside, or after three to four weeks of cold, wet treatment in the refrigerator. Seedlings from this species had grown small rosettes of leaves by May and were potted on into larger pots. By the end of July their well-grown leaves resembled those of garden hybrids (see **Figure 11.11a**). Most of the seedlings were reluctant to flower in their first season, but a few produced a central flowering stem in mid-August. The plants were tall, nearly 1 metre (39 inches) in height, with a very narrow spike and a large number (about 70) of tiny florets (see **Figure 11.11b**). These florets were upright and remained cupped, being greenish-white

LEFT: **Figure 11.11b.** The long, narrow flower spike of *D. californicum* subsp. *interius* bears curious greeny-yellow florets with pronounced pink tinges.

FAR LEFT: **Figure 11.11a.** Foliage of *D. californicum* subsp. *interius* resembles that of garden hybrid delphiniums.

with a distinct pink tinge to the eye. A number of plants, either over-wintered in the ground or in pots that were kept dry, survived to flower in the following August or September. To us, the interesting point about this species delphinium was that the dormant crown, like that of garden hybrids, produces large crown buds. However, the florets are so small that this species does not appear to offer any hybridization potential.

The examples we have given of delphinium species requiring a period of cold, wet treatment have all germinated within six weeks. There are other species that are more demanding and need 12 or more weeks before they will appear. This is not difficult utilizing a refrigerator, but the timing of this period is less easy to manage. These plants need to reach a sufficient size before dormancy, and often all that they will produce in their first season is a single stem topped by twin cotyledons. All need to be started in the early winter of the previous year, or left in compost over the summer to undergo a further full cold period. A general indication that this long cold period will be required can be obtained by considering the natural habitat in which they evolved: species growing at altitudes in excess of 2,500 metres (8,200 feet) have adapted to survive harsh winter conditions. This group includes *D. andersonii, barbeyi, geyeri, nelsonii, nuttallianum,* and *glaucum.* The last-named we have grown successfully to flower, and this species, found in wet sites in sub-alpine meadows, resembles garden hybrids in leaf form and general appearance, but the dark blue-purple florets are very small.

Do try and grow some of these species – or any others that we have not mentioned – if the seed becomes available to you. Remember that unless the seed is collected in the wild, you may be offered seed that is of hybrid origin or is wrongly named, so do try to check your plants against descriptions in books or in the *Flora,* or by using the internet. We are sure you will get a great deal of satisfaction in growing some of these delphiniums in your garden.

Growing Annual Larkspurs

It is important to realize that seeds derived from species of *Consolida* will not germinate satisfactorily when sown in hot weather, since they require temperatures around 8–14°C (46–57°F). It is advisable to place seeds on wet paper kitchen towel in lidded boxes in the refrigerator for three weeks before sowing, however, since given this pre-treatment, they will germinate at higher temperatures. Because of this need for cool conditions during germination, larkspurs are often sown during the autumn when aiming for large plants that flower in May and June. Further sowings in March and April will give flowers in August to September – around 20 weeks after sowing. As these garden forms are derived from plants originating in poor soils or grasslands, they are fairly tolerant of soil type. However, autumn sowings should not be made in very heavy or wet soils. If you have these conditions, it is better to sow seed in fibre, peat or small plastic pots and keep them in a cold frame over the winter. They can be transplanted in spring with minimal disturbance. Spring sowings after chilling the seed should be made in the place where the plants are to flower so as to avoid transplanting, because seedlings can quickly grow 'leggy' unless they are grown under optimum conditions of light.

If you are growing larkspurs in rows to be used for cut flowers, allow at least 45 centimetres (18 inches) between the rows because the individual plants will get quite large. Thin within the rows at intervals as their growth increases, removing the weakest plants. Like their cousins, these plants are vulnerable to the attentions of slugs and snails, and also to powdery mildew. The entire plant can rapidly become white, and the appearance of the flower spike ruined, with this fungus, so preventative sprays must be used. With their numerous branches bearing flowers, larkspurs quickly become top-heavy and must be supported by twiggy sticks through which they can grow, or with canes and twine.

Appendices

Registration of Delphinium Names

If a selected delphinium cultivar is considered suitable to be given a name, it is desirable that the name is included in The International Delphinium Register. This Register also includes names given to seed lines (selections) intended for distribution.

Registration forms can be obtained from:

The International Delphinium Registrar
RHS Garden
Wisley
Woking
Surrey GU23 6QB
UK

or from the RHS website at:

www.rhs.org.uk/plants/registration.asp

There is no fee for basic registration or for the certificate (if this is requested). The registration form requires information about the plant, such as the shape and size of leaves, length of flower spike, size and form of flowers and length of pedicels. The colour of the flowers must be described, preferably in terms of colours in the RHS Colour Chart, and it is advisable to supply good photographs of the flowers. For registration, the plant should preferably differ from other named cultivars, and it is essential that the name be unique. Since the register contains so many names, it is always a good idea to check the suitability of a proposed name with the registrar before submitting a formal application for registration. One strategy widely used to ensure a chosen name will be acceptable is to add a prefix specific to the plant raiser. For example, we used 'Summerfield' (a house name) as the prefix for several cultivars that we introduced, to ensure that their name is unique.

Plant Breeders' Rights

Name registration confers no legal rights of plant ownership to the person registering the name. In contrast, the granting of plant breeders' rights confers legal rights to the applicant. The owner of the rights can then demand royalty payments on any material of the cultivar that is propagated for sale. Plant Breeders' Rights are granted only after a 'DUS Test' ensures that the stock of the cultivar is distinct from any other named cultivar available in cultivation, is uniform in character, is genetically stable and free from disease. Substantial fees are charged for the DUS test, and annually thereafter for the maintenance of the rights, once a grant rights has been made. Applications for rights are therefore not appropriate unless it is likely that the cultivar will be propagated for commercial sale on a very large scale, for example by micropropagation.

In Britain, Plant Breeders' Rights are administered by:

The Plant Variety Rights Office
White House Lane
Huntingdon Road
Cambridge CB3 0LF
UK

Information can be obtained from the following website:

www.defra.gov.uk/planth/pvs/guides/pbrguide-20050317.pdf

Equivalent rights applicable throughout the European Union are obtainable and similar schemes for plant patents operate in the United States and other countries.

Award of Garden Merit

Delphinium Trials have been in progress at the Royal Horticultural Society's Garden, Wisley since 1916. Since 1993, the purpose of the Trials has been the assessment of cultivars for the Award of Garden Merit (AGM). Following a preliminary examination by the Delphinium Committee, any cultivars submitted by individuals and nursery people are grown in the gardens along with a selection of AGM cultivars as control standards. Entries are judged when the flowers are well developed, to assess their value for garden decoration. To ensure that AGM cultivars perform consistently despite variations in weather conditions from year to year, entries in the trial are awarded an AGM only if they have been judged to be of the required standard in three seasons, although not necessarily in consecutive years. Trials of delphiniums from seed are also carried out from time to time.

Information about the Trials of Delphiniums can be obtained from the RHS website:

www.rhs.org.uk/trials

or by contacting:

The Trials Office
RHS Garden
Wisley
Woking
Surrey GU23 6QB
UK

email: **trials@rhs.org.uk**

The Delphinium Society

This specialist plant society, founded in 1928, exists to promote interest in all aspects of delphinium cultivation, and has an international membership. The society publishes annually a yearbook that provides information on cultivation methods, items of topical interest and colour photographs of delphinium cultivars. Past issues are generally available from the Delphinium Society. The society has no permanent office, and information on contact details should be obtained from an internet search or from the Royal Horticultural Society at:

www.rhs.org.uk

Index